THE
CHRISTIAN
COUNSELOR'S
HANDBOOK

THE
CHRISTIAN
COUNSELOR'S
HANDBOOK

The Topical Handbook Used by the Prayer-Counselors of
THE CHRISTIAN BROADCASTING NETWORK

 The Christian Broadcasting Network Virginia Beach, Virginia
Tyndale House Publishers, Inc. Wheaton, Illinois

Library of Congress
Catalog Card Number
87-50069
ISBN 0-8423-0255-7

CONTENTS

This book is the distillation of the experiences our counselors have had in ministering to 25 million people on the telephones during the last quarter of a century.

Since our first broadcast day, on October 1, 1961, our vision has remained the same—to reach a hurting world for Christ. And by God's grace we are doing just that.

For these many years now, dedicated and loving CBN counselors have continued to sit faithfully by the telephones. They are ready to minister to the thousands who call every day with every sort of problem, from abortion, to divorce and family problems, to depression, to drugs, to suicide.

As God increased CBN's ability to minister by telephone and person-to-person to millions each year, it became apparent that if we were to remain true to our calling, our counselors had to be better equipped.

This ready-reference handbook of the Bible's answers to people's problems and needs was God's answer to our need. This edition of *The Christian Counselor's Handbook* is the result of hundreds of hours of research, experience, careful planning, prayer, and humble seeking of God's wisdom.

It was a monumental task. But the Holy Spirit enabled it. I know it will bless you. I have seen the miraculous results as the book was used. In this book you will find the answers that our counselors use to minister to people who will make over 5 million telephone calls to us this year.

Use this book in your personal life. Use it to counsel others.

It works. It will work for you tomorrow as well as it does today. The truths of God's Word in this book will not change. Those truths will stand though heaven and earth pass away.

Pat Robertson, Chairman of the Board, Chief Executive Officer
The Christian Broadcasting Network, Inc.

The Christian Counselor's Handbook was prepared as a reference and guide especially for counselors of the Christian Broadcasting Network, Inc. It is a supplement to other manuals, books, and counseling aids which may be more extensive in their treatment of each subject. Tens of thousands of counselors have used the handbook for personal ministry and at the many CBN 700 Club Centers around the world. It has aided in ministering to the millions of people who have called for prayer and biblical counsel since its introduction in 1978.

The need for the handbook was recognized and conceived in December 1976. The handbook is the result of literally hundreds of aggregate years of prayer, Bible study, experience, and Holy Spirit-inspired wisdom of some thirty CBN 700 Club Center Managers. There were at least four ministers who worked both individually, then on committee, to produce the material for each subject. They completed their work in August 1977. The handbook was then submitted to fifteen ministers, 700 Club Center Managers, and trained Christian counselors. They critically evaluated it as to form, Scriptures applied, doctrines, and usefulness in counseling and for teaching. It was then rewritten, edited, and rewritten again.

We have attempted to give guidance in "how" to overcome problems as well as to analyze and show "why" a problem occurs. The counseling approach has been to give positive, directive counsel on how to correct problems in one's life as the Holy Spirit reveals his wisdom to the counselor. The fight against Satan and evil is one of facing him squarely, with the authority and power of God in the Holy Spirit, to chase Satan and never retreat. He is a defeated enemy, and the Christian counselor is more than conqueror in Christ.

Rather than being *the* way to counsel and pray, the handbook presents one way and a basis from which to minister. It presupposes that a counselor is already a born-again Christian. We believe and have experienced that the baptism with the Holy Spirit makes a Christian more truly effective as he seeks both to live a victorious and overcoming life in Christ, and as he ministers to others (Acts 1:8). A person who counsels should continue to receive more in-depth training and practical experience than it is possible to gain from this handbook alone. The handbook is meant for one who is *becoming* a Christian counselor, as he grows spiritually in the Lord under inspiration of the Holy Spirit.

Our prayer is that you will be blessed, that the anointing of the Holy Spirit will be upon you as you study and use the handbook, and that souls will be saved and God glorified as a result of this work.

Do:
1. Pray without ceasing, giving thanks and praise in all circumstances.
2. Listen prayerfully to the counselee. Expect the Spirit to reveal what you are to speak, pray about, or do for each counselee. It may or may not be what is requested.
3. When counseling, quote biblical passages that speak to the problem: both those that analyze and those that make positive approaches to overcoming or being victorious.
4. Always be courteous and helpful. Recognize that the counselee is speaking with you with hope that you will help.
5. Act with all the authority Jesus gives. Be firm against Satan. Speak directly to the problem rather than about it, around it, etc. Don't say what you are going to do; do it in the name of Jesus.
6. Keep any commitments you make; e.g., follow through on a promise.
7. Become very familiar with the principles of AGREEMENT/DISAGREE-MENT, FASTING, PRAISE, FAVOR, GIVING AND TITHING, and INTERCESSION (see individual sections). These apply in most of the solutions you will need to offer in counseling. Encourage counselees to learn and practice them.
8. Always, even if all else fails, be a channel of *love*.
9. Expect God to answer your prayers with signs accompanying the gifts of the Holy Spirit.

Do Not:
1. Argue, condemn, criticize, preach, "talk down to," or overreact and talk loudly.
2. Proselyte (from one church to another) or counsel someone to leave their church (unless it is an occult or non-Christian religious group).
3. Counsel someone to stop taking medicine or not see a doctor. That is a decision you cannot make.
4. Counsel someone to get a divorce or leave a spouse; i.e., never give counsel contrary to Scripture.
5. Dictate what counselee is to do. Rather, suggest. Counselee must make his own decisions.

"As far as I am concerned about you, my brothers, I am convinced that you especially are abounding in highest goodness, richly supplied with perfect *knowledge* and *competent to counsel* one another" (Rom. 15:14, WMS).

As Christian counselors we serve as comforters to those who are suffering, helpers to those in need, advocates who process the advice and guidance from the Scriptures in our own lives and pass it on.

To share another's suffering in silent prayer (as he talks about his problems) is much better than trying to argue with him about theological matters. We need to know also that we are never working alone. The Holy Spirit directs; the counselors counsel (John 14:16).

HOW TO USE THIS HANDBOOK
The handbook has been designed so that every opportunity to counsel is maximized. Though designed primarily for telephone counseling, personal face-to-face ministry will be aided as you learn to use the handbook. You should restrain yourself from reading directly from the handbook as you are talking to the counselee. Rather, it should be used as a reference during the counseling session.

Topics included represent the most common problems people face today. Almost from the first during a discussion with a counselee, you may begin to discern to which topics you should turn. Often you may need to turn to two or three as they apply to a person's needs.

Counseling steps often follow the following outline:

1. Stop, look, and listen to the counselee.
2. Identify the main problem.
3. Share Scripture and counsel.
4. Ask for a response.
5. Follow through with prayer and ministry as need is discerned.
6 Give homework and refer to a pastor as needed.

PROBLEM-SOLVING PROCESSES
Avoid the temptation to provide overly simple solutions for complex problems. Simplicity is needed, but be wary of oversimplification. Quite often in our culture we have answers before we know the questions, and solutions before we understand the problems. Every problem is unique, but there are certain general patterns that can be observed:

1. Problems of a personal nature never exist in total isolation.
2. The conditions that later may be designated as "a personal problem" often exist long before these factors are known.
3. Conditioning by our culture, subcultures, and social situations influences our awareness of personal problems. A sick man in a sick society may feel in perfect health, until he or his social conditions change. This is the point at which a person might ask for counsel.
4. The statement of a problem is important. The counselor must hear not just the words but the sound of the voice for major clues to a problem.
5. When a person asks for assistance with personal problems, half the victory is already won. Here is where a counselor needs to exercise restraint and listen.
6. Jesus Christ, when he was confronted by people with problems, focused on the most important problem. This should be our Christian counseling methodology.
7. One of the most common problems in counseling is a predisposition to counsel with one favorite solution for all problems. Avoid this single solution syndrome. Learn to hear the Holy Spirit speaking.
8. The solution should be from the guidance of the Holy Spirit (John 16:13, 14), who might also reveal other problems that may be implicit in the situation.

SPIRIT-LED COUNSELING

The Holy Spirit is the one that brings about the change in people for the better. What we have to offer is prayer and counsel as the Holy Spirit brings it to our minds (John 14:26). In this handbook are specific Scripture verses that apply to the defined situations. We need to have the Scripture in our hearts and minds for the Holy Spirit to be able to call it up from memory when needed. After listening to the counselee's problem or need, and before any counsel, advice, or even Scripture is shared, the counselor should pray either silently or with the counselee. As silent or shared verbal praise and thanksgiving is offered (Eph. 5:20; 1 Thess. 5:18), the Holy Spirit will begin to bring to mind how to pray, what to say, and what to do (Prov. 16:3; John 14:26; John 16:12-15).

The counselor should counsel according to applicable Scripture. It is not advice per se that is needed, but God's Word applied to the need. God's Word will accomplish the work he sends it to do (Isa. 55:11).

Good common sense, God-given wisdom, knowledge, and the guidance of the Holy Spirit is what we need for Christian counseling. What makes us "competent to counsel"? It is the working of God in us and in those we have an opportunity to help.

COUNSELING GOAL

The goal in counseling is always to help the counselee help himself. He needs to press on to maturity and toward being an overcomer. With this in mind, the primary emphases with which any Christian counselor is concerned are (1) salvation, (2) water baptism, (3) baptism with the Holy Spirit, (4) maturing and manifesting the fruit of the Spirit, (5) putting on the full armor of God, (6) spiritual edification as the principles of the Kingdom of God are learned and practiced, (7) personal ministry from and participation in the ministry of prophets, apostles, evangelists, pastors, and teachers, and (8) personal ministry through the gifts and power of the Holy Spirit. In all these areas, the counselee should be referred to a local Christ-centered church that clearly teaches the Bible for further follow-up ministry where personal growth, fellowship, and any further counsel can be received.

To help him mature spiritually, the counselee needs to follow through in his search for help. He needs to "do his homework." The references and homework section of each subject list some books and Bible passages. Others may be available from the counselor's own experience and study. Strongly urge the counselee to do some self-help study.

ABUSE

SCRIPTURE

Romans 3:23
Yes, all have sinned; all fall short of God's glorious ideal.

Romans 5:8
But God showed his great love for us by sending Christ to die for us while we were still sinners.

John 3:17
God did not send his Son into the world to condemn it, but to save it.

Proverbs 28:13
A man who refuses to admit his mistakes can never be successful. But if he confesses and forsakes them, he gets another chance.

1 John 1:8, 9
If we say that we have no sin, we are only fooling ourselves, and refusing to accept the truth. But if we confess our sins to him, he can be depended on to forgive us and to cleanse us from every wrong. [And it is perfectly proper for God to do this for us because Christ died to wash away our sins.]

John 8:32, 36
And you will know the truth, and the truth will set you free. So if the Son sets you free, you will indeed be free.

PROBLEM

An alcoholic is one who is not able to control his desire for alcoholic beverages, and consequently consumes excessive amounts. His personality traits and the problem areas of his life are intensified. In an effort to cover up his inadequacies, he will tend to overcompensate in everything he does. He may drink on the job and even need a drink to "get going" in the morning. Every area of his life will be affected by his uncontrollable desire to drink.

BIBLICAL PERSPECTIVE

God is able to help the alcoholic. Referring to drunkards, Paul wrote, "There was a time when some of you were just like that but now your sins are washed away, and you were set apart for God, and he has accepted you because of what the Lord Jesus Christ and the Spirit of our God have done for you" (1 Cor. 6:11). Alcohol abuse is the result of following our own wrong inclinations (Gal. 5:19-21), but the Holy Spirit is able to control our lives and produce in us the self-control needed to overcome alcoholism (Gal. 5:22, 23).

COUNSEL

Once the alcoholic has stopped drinking, he must never taste it again, not even in moderation. To some that may sound like an extreme view, an over-generalization. But in countless cases it has been proven that an alcoholic cannot drink intoxicating beverages without becoming enslaved again. So the counselor's goal must be to help the alcoholic adopt a mind-set and life-style of total abstinence.

For the most part the alcoholic feels condemned already, so don't try to shame him into sobriety. He already knows *why* he shouldn't drink, but doesn't know *how* to stop. Don't condemn, but urge the alcoholic to be reconciled to God. Show him the promises in God's Word that Jesus Christ offers love, forgiveness, inner peace, and goodness. What a privilege God has given us to share his kind of good news with those who so desperately need it (2 Cor. 5:17-21).

Once he has put his trust in Christ for the forgiveness of sins, shower him with Christian love and share with him Scripture verses which will assure him that Christ is now living in his heart (examples: John 6:45; 2 Cor. 5:17; Rev. 3:20).

This new Christian life, especially the idea of total abstinence, may seem overwhelming to him. He has made promises many times to God, to himself, and to family that he would never drink again, so now he wonders if it will be any different this time.

You must teach him how to live one day at a time, with the power of the Holy Spirit. He needs to remain sober today and be successful in his new walk with Christ. Then again tomorrow and the next day. Each day of victory will give him courage and strength to face the days ahead. This is the beginning of a new life.

Certainly a change in life-style is the goal, but that will only come as he changes his thinking habits. When counseling the alcoholic who has accepted Christ, emphasize what Jesus said: "Apart from me you can't do a thing." Encourage the new believer to rely on the power of the Holy Spirit at all times, study and obey the Bible, and faithfully attend a church where he can ". . . grow in spiritual strength and become better acquainted with our Lord and Savior Jesus Christ . . ." (2 Pet. 3:18).

Urge family and friends to refrain from ever

2 Corinthians 5:17
When someone becomes a Christian he becomes a brand new person inside. He is not the same any more. A new life has begun!

Galatians 5:22, 23
But when the Holy Spirit controls our lives he will produce this kind of fruit in us: love, joy, peace, patience, kindness, goodness, faithfulness, gentleness and self-control. . . .

Romans 12:2
Don't copy the behavior and customs of this world, but be a new and different person with a fresh newness in all you do and think.

Philippians 4:8
Fix your thoughts on what is true and good and right. Think about things that are pure and lovely, and dwell on the fine, good things in others. Think about all you can praise God for and be glad about.

1 Thessalonians 5:16-18
Always be joyful. Always keep on praying. No matter what happens, always be thankful, for this is God's will for you who belong to Christ Jesus.

Hebrews 13:15
With Jesus' help we will continually offer our sacrifice of praise to God by telling others of the glory of his name.

REFERENCES

2 Timothy 2:11-13
Life is tough, but God is faithful

Philippians 3:12-14
Forget the past and look forward

Psalm 103
God forgives, forgets, and supports

Isaiah 40:27-31
God gives strength to the weak

John 8:34-36
The Son of God sets you free

Galatians 5:22, 23
Fruit of the Spirit growing in you

Romans 10:17
How to get more faith

Romans 8:31-37
God is on your side

_____

_____

_____

_____

_____

_____

_____

_____

_____

_____

_____

condemning the alcoholic. Refer them to a church for Christian fellowship or to ALANON, where they will find encouragement and fellowship with the friends and relatives of other alcoholics. Remind them that now, more than ever, the alcoholic needs their daily support. Encourage the alcoholic to seek help through a Christian treatment program or to join AA and also to become involved in a supportive church.

PRAYER

Pray that the alcoholic will forsake his compulsive life-style and learn self-discipline and careful obedience to God's Word. Pray that he will be delivered from his psychological and physical dependence on alcohol and even that desire for just one drink. Pray that his fear of failure will be replaced by perfect peace. "He will keep in perfect peace all those who trust in him, whose thoughts turn often to the Lord! Trust in the Lord God always, for in the Lord Jehovah is your everlasting strength" (Isa. 26:3, 4).

FOLLOW-UP

1. Remember that God has forgiven you and that sin no longer has control of your life.
2. Be prepared to refuse a drink, because the temptation will come.
3. Don't believe that thought that keeps going through your mind: "If I can have just one drink I'll be able to make it through the day."
4. Repeat to yourself and others: "With God's help, I'm not going to have a drink today."
5. Join together with other Christians to study the Bible and pray. That support and fellow-ship will get you through.
6. Read, study, and memorize the Bible on your

own. Remember that God's "words are a flashlight to light the path ahead of me, and keep me from stumbling" (Ps. 119:105).

7. All day long keep praying and praising God for the way he is demonstrating his power in your life. "Is anything too hard for God?" (Gen. 18:14). "What can we ever say to such wonderful things as these? If God is on our side, who can ever be against us? Since he did not spare even his own Son for us but gave him up for us all, won't he also surely give us everything else?" (Rom. 8:31, 32).

8. If God has forgiven you, and he did when you trusted him, now do like Paul, "forgetting the past and looking forward to what lies ahead . . . " (Phil. 3:13).

9. When you go back on your word to God and sin against him in any way, turn to the promise in 1 John 1:9 and confess your sins to him.

10. Begin a balanced diet and suitable exercise program (supervised by a doctor).

SCRIPTURE

Proverbs 19:11
A wise man restrains his anger and overlooks insults. This is to his credit.

Luke 17:1-3
"There will always be temptations to sin," Jesus said one day to his disciples, "but woe to the man who does the tempting. If he were thrown into the sea with a huge rock tied to his neck, he would be far better off than facing the punishment in store for those who harm these little children's souls. I am warning you!

"Rebuke your brother if he sins, and forgive him if he is sorry."

1 Corinthians 13:4-7
Love is patient and kind, never jealous or envious, never boastful or proud, never haughty or selfish or rude. Love does not demand its own way. It is not irritable or touchy. It does not hold grudges and will hardly even notice when others do it wrong. It is never glad about injustice, but rejoices whenever truth wins out. If you love someone you will be loyal to him no matter what the cost. You will always believe in him, always expect the best of him, and always stand your ground in defending him.

PROBLEM

Most of us love children, but sometimes those precious little ones get on our nerves and we lose patience. It happens to the best of us. But there are some adults who become abnormally angry and overreact, hurting the child emotionally and physically.

In order to deal with this problem, it is important that we understand the difference between child abuse and discipline. According to *Black's Law Dictionary,* child abuse is "any form of cruelty to a child's physical, moral, or mental well-being," whereas, according to Dr. James Dobson in *Dare to Discipline,* discipline is "a function of love" (pg. 29). He states that "children thrive best in an atmosphere of genuine love, undergirded by reasonable, consistent discipline" (pg. 13). So child abuse is cruel, while discipline is reasonable and loving.

BIBLICAL PERSPECTIVE

Since children are a gift from the Lord (Ps. 127:3), a parent should be careful that he does not scold and nag so much that his child becomes angry, resentful, and discouraged. Instead, he should give him that kind of discipline which meets the approval of the Lord (Eph. 6:4; Col. 3:21).

COUNSEL

In many cases the child abuser was himself abused as a child. So now he abuses children for possibly two reasons: he learned this abnormal behavior in childhood, and now has no model to imitate but the adult who abused him; and he may be filled with such frustration and anger from childhood that he now takes it out on innocent children. That sounds ironic, but it is all too common.

Certainly the first thing you can do for this person is explain to him how he can know God's forgiveness and make Jesus Christ his Savior and Lord. "When someone becomes a Christian he becomes a brand new person inside. He is not the same any more. A new life has begun!" (2 Cor. 5:17).

Alcoholism may be the cause of his rage and can be dealt with according to the counsel found in the section in this book on ALCOHOLISM.

Here are three steps to help the child abuser overcome his problem:

1. Recognize that child abuse is a sin (1 John 1:8, 10), and that by simply confessing the sin to God, you can experience forgiveness and cleansing (1 John 1:9).
2. Forgive those who have abused you—those who were cruel to you in childhood and those who are now making you frustrated and angry (Matt. 6:14, 15).
3. Be filled with the Holy Spirit and be controlled by him (Eph. 5:18; Gal. 5:22, 23).

Remind the child abuser that what he has done is against the law. Show him what God says about breaking the laws of government (Rom. 13:1-3; 1 Pet. 2:13, 14).

PRAYER

Encourage the abuser to ask both God and the abused child for their forgiveness. Help him to thank the Lord that he loves him, that he forgives, and even makes us his children. Pray that God will change the child abuser's life and attitudes, and that the Holy Spirit will produce in him all the love, joy, peace, patience, kindness, goodness, faithfulness, gentleness, and self-

Galatians 5:22, 23
But when the Holy Spirit controls our lives he will produce this kind of fruit in us: love, joy, peace, patience, kindness, goodness, faithfulness, gentleness and self-control.

Ephesians 4:26, 27
If you are angry, don't sin by nursing your grudge. Don't let the sun go down with you still angry—get over it quickly: for when you are angry you give a mighty foothold to the devil.

Ephesians 6:4
And now a word to you parents. Don't keep on scolding and nagging your children, making them angry and resentful. Rather, bring them up with the loving discipline the Lord himself approves, with suggestions and godly advice.

Colossians 3:8
But now is the time to cast off and throw away all these rotten garments of anger, hatred, cursing, and dirty language.

Colossians 3:2
Let heaven fill your thoughts; don't spend your time worrying about things down here.

control needed to overcome the temptation to abuse children.

REFERENCES

Romans 6
Sin's power has been broken by Christ

Romans 12:1, 2
You can be a new person in all you think and do

1 Corinthians 10:13
No temptation is irresistible; God will show you how to escape its power

Ephesians 6:1-18
Put on God's armor to stand against Satan's tricks

Philippians 4:8, 9, 13
Fix your mind on good things and Christ will help you

James 4:7
Give yourself to God and you will be able to resist the devil

Jude 24, 25
God can keep you from slipping and falling again

PROBLEM

Habitual use of narcotic, stimulant, or mind-influencing drugs for nonmedical purposes. May involve physical and/or psychological addiction. Has its roots as a sin problem, causing spiritual enslavement and depravity. (See the section on ALCOHOLISM.)

BIBLICAL PERSPECTIVE

Jesus Christ came to release those who are captive and to help people gain self-control, which is a fruit of the Spirit (Gal. 5:22, 23).

COUNSEL

Realize that the drug user or addict feels imprisoned by the problem; he is truly a captive, in bondage. You can stimulate in them a sense of hope simply by expressing your concern and God's care.

Some say it takes thirty-one days to break a habit. Drug addiction pervades the life of the user, so radical changes must be made regarding his association with friends, involvement with social groups, and participation in activities surrounded by drugs and other drug users. The first step you should take is to put the counselee in touch with a helping group or agency. Recommend a church, Bible study, or prayer group for Christian fellowship that is Christ-centered and clearly teaches the Bible. Try to arrange a contact between the counselee and a Christian friend.

The counselee needs to keep busy and occupy his mind with new things (Phil. 4:8, 9). Remind him that he must yield himself to Christ rather than to his old associations. Present to him salvation and the power of the Holy Spirit to change his life.

SCRIPTURE

1 Corinthians 6:12
I can do anything I want to if Christ has not said no, but some of these things aren't good for me. Even if I am allowed to do them, I'll refuse to if I think they might get such a grip on me that I can't easily stop when I want to.

Ephesians 5:18
Don't drink too much wine, for many evils lie along that path; be filled instead with the Holy Spirit, and controlled by him.

Luke 4:18
He has sent me to heal the brokenhearted and to announce that captives shall be released and the blind shall see.

Colossians 2:15
In this way God took away Satan's power to accuse you of sin, and God openly displayed to the whole world Christ's triumph at the cross where your sins were all taken away.

1 John 3:8
But if you keep on sinning, it shows that you belong to Satan, who since he first began to sin has kept steadily at it. But the Son of God came to destroy these works of the devil.

Galatians 5:1, 13
So Christ has made us free. Now make sure that you stay free and don't get all tied up again in the chains of slavery. . . . For, dear brothers, you have been given freedom: not freedom to do wrong, but freedom to love and serve each other.

REFERENCES

Romans 11:2
God does not reject his chosen ones

Philippians 4:4-9
Growth in Christ

PRAYER

Pray for Christ to deliver the drug user from his sin. Thank God for his love, concern, and power to deliver the counselee from the problem. Have the counselee pray the following: I now choose to let go of the drugs, my old friends, and my old hangouts. I give myself to you, Lord Jesus. Come into my heart and fill me with your Holy Spirit. I take you at your word and thank you for delivering me from drugs and my desire for them. Thank you for freeing me. Amen.

FOLLOW-UP

Start to heal the broken relationships in your life. Forgive those who have hurt you. Apologize to those you've hurt.

Set up a regular, everyday Bible reading plan. Start out each new day with prayer. Attend church. Seek fellowship with other Christians.

READING
The Cross and the Switchblade by David Wilkerson
The Jesus Pocket Promise Book by David Wilkerson
Run Baby Run by Nicky Cruz

PROBLEM

The counselee may be enslaved by the desire to smoke, caught in the trap of this unhealthy habit. Or he may be trying to cut down or quit and in need of encouragement and strength in his resolve.

BIBLICAL PERSPECTIVE

It is not what goes into a person that defiles him, but what comes out of his mouth. However, when one is in bondage to a physical addiction, it can lead to all kinds of psychological and spiritual damage as well. What destroys the body is harming our temple, which is where God's Spirit desires to dwell (1 Cor. 6:19, 20; 2 Pet. 2:19; Rom. 6:12). A Christian who smokes also may offend weaker Christians and damage his witness (1 Cor. 8:7-13; Rom. 15:1-3).

COUNSEL

Do not condemn or criticize the smoker, but help him to turn his problem over to Christ for healing. Pray for his deliverance—physically, mentally, and spiritually. He needs to concentrate in his prayers on curbing desire for the habit. When each temptation to smoke comes, he should affirm: "I am not going to smoke right now."

In order to distract himself from the desire to smoke, he should begin occupying his mind with God and his Word, spending time in conscious worship. He should begin to praise God instead of dwelling on the smoking problem.

The counselee should replace his former habit with a healthful one, such as a mild exercise program or other activity. He should consult his doctor about exercise, especially if he is older.

SCRIPTURE

1 Corinthians 6:19, 20
Haven't you yet learned that your body is the home of the Holy Spirit God gave you and that he lives within you? Your own body does not belong to you.

2 Peter 2:19
"You aren't saved by being good," they say, "so you might as well be bad. Do what you like, be free." But these very teachers who offer this "freedom" from law are themselves slaves to sin and destruction. For a man is a slave to whatever controls him.

Romans 15:1-3
Even if we believe that it makes no difference to the Lord whether we do these things, still we cannot just go ahead and do them to please ourselves; for we must bear the "burden" of being considerate of the doubts and fears of others—of those who feel these things are wrong. Let's please the other fellow, not ourselves, and do what is for his good and thus build him up in the Lord. Christ didn't please himself. As the Psalmist said, "He came for the very purpose of suffering under the insults of those who were against the Lord."

Romans 6:12
*Do not let sin control your
puny body any longer; do not
give in to its sinful desires.*

PRAYER

Thank and praise God for delivering the counselee from the desire to smoke. Thank God for
cleansing and forgiving the counselee.

REFERENCES

1 John 5:4, 5
Victory in Christ

Philippians 4:13
Victory in Christ

1 John 4:4
Victory in Christ

1 Corinthians 10:13
God is faithful

Psalm 22:3
Enthrone him in praise

Hebrews 13:15
Praise to God

ATTITUDES

SCRIPTURE

Exodus 20:17
You must not be envious of your neighbor's house, or want to sleep with his wife, or want to own his slaves, oxen, donkeys, or anything else he has.

Matthew 26:41
Keep alert and pray. Otherwise temptation will overpower you. For the spirit indeed is willing, but how weak the body is!

1 Corinthians 13:4
Love is very patient and kind, never jealous or envious, never boastful or proud, never haughty or selfish or rude. Love does not demand its own way. It is not irritable or touchy. It does not hold grudges and will hardly even notice when others do it wrong.

Philippians 4:8
And now brothers, as I close this letter let me say this one more thing: Fix your thoughts on what is true and good and right. Think about things that are pure and lovely, and dwell on the fine, good things in others. Think about all you can praise God for and be glad about.

James 5:16
Admit your faults to one another and pray for each other so that you may be healed. The earnest prayer of a righteous man has great power and wonderful results.

PROBLEM

Covetousness, that excessive desire for what belongs to someone else, is a secret sin that can dominate your thinking and eventually control your actions. Unchecked, covetousness will lead to theft, adultery, and murder.

BIBLICAL PERSPECTIVE

God commands us not to be envious of what belongs to someone else (Exod. 20:17).

COUNSEL

We tend to categorize sins and even minimize their gravity. But God hates all sin and cannot allow it in his presence. Therefore, covetousness, like any other sin, must be confessed and forsaken. And a plan must be devised and put into motion that will counteract every temptation to covet.

Here are six steps you can take to overcome covetousness:

Confess to God that you have sinned against him by being envious. Then he will forgive and cleanse you of all wrong (1 John 1:8-10).

Stop envying. Of course, that's easier said than done, but you must willfully stop doing what you know is sin (Heb. 13:4, 5).

Learn the secret of contentment. Jesus Christ can help you to live happily with what you have; he will strengthen you (Phil. 4:11-13). To learn the secret of contentment, become a truly thankful person: "Always be joyful. Always keep on praying. No matter what happens, always be thankful, for this is God's will for you who belong to Christ Jesus" (1 Thess. 5:16).

Give to others in need. The best defense is a good offense. So, to combat covetousness, give generously to others, since covetousness is simply committing theft in your mind. Paul's instructions found in Ephesians 4:28 should be applied: "If anyone is stealing he must stop it and begin using those hands of his for honest work so he can give to others in need." Freely giving to others will nip covetousness in the bud.

Fix your thoughts on what is true and good and right (Phil. 4:8). Covetousness is a sin which is committed in the heart and mind. Therefore, it is important that the mind be filled with good thoughts to displace covetousness before it manifests itself in sinful acts such as theft, adultery, and murder.

Pray for the person you envy (Matt. 26:41; James 5:16). When you pray for someone, you are demonstrating that you really love and care for him, and at the same time you are strengthening that love. Your loving prayers for the person you envy will soon win over your excessive desire for what does not belong to you (1 Cor. 13:4).

' PRAYER

Pray that the counselee's covetousness will be replaced by love and contentment, and will not have a chance to develop into theft, adultery, or murder.

REFERENCES

Psalm 119:36, 37
Prefer obedience to God over making money

1 Corinthians 10:24
Think about what is best for others, not just yourself

Galatians 5:22, 23
Let the Holy Spirit control your life

Hebrews 13:15, 16
Praise God for his goodness and share what you have with those in need

1 John 1:9
Confess your covetousness to God

Philippians 4:11-13
Not that I was ever in need, for I have learned how to get along happily whether I have much or little. I know how to live on almost nothing or with everything. I have learned the secret of contentment in every situation, whether it be a full stomach or hunger, plenty or want. For I can do everything God asks me to with the help of Christ who gives the strength and power.

Hebrews 13:4, 5
Honor your marriage and its vows, and be pure; for God will surely punish all those who are immoral or commit adultery.

Stay away from the love of money; be satisfied with what you have. For God has said, "I will never, never fail you nor forsake you."

1 John 1:8-10
If we say that we have no sin, we are only fooling ourselves, and refusing to accept the truth. But if we confess our sins to him, he can be depended on to forgive us and to cleanse us from every wrong. [And it is perfectly proper for God to do this for us because Christ died to wash away our sins.] If we claim we have not sinned, we are lying and calling God a liar, for he says we have sinned.

SCRIPTURE

Exodus 23:4, 5
If you come upon an enemy's ox or donkey that has strayed away, you must take it back to its owner. If you see your enemy trying to get his donkey onto its feet beneath a heavy load, you must not go on by, but must help him.

Proverbs 24:17, 18
Do not rejoice when your enemy meets trouble. Let there be no gladness when he falls—for the Lord may be displeased with you and stop punishing him!

Luke 6:27-37
Listen, all of you. Love your enemies. Do good to those who hate you. Pray for the happiness of those who curse you, implore God's blessing on those who hurt you.

If someone slaps you on one cheek, let him slap the other too! If someone demands your coat, give him your shirt besides. Give what you have to anyone who asks you for it; and when things are taken away from you, don't worry about getting them back. Treat others as you want them to treat you.

Do you think you deserve credit for merely loving those who love you? Even the godless do that! And if you do good only to those who do you good—is that so wonderful? Even sinners do that much! And if you lend money only to those who can repay you,

PROBLEM

Inability to cope with a person who represents a threat, or who manifests hostile opposition in some way. God's love and peace are not effectually present in one who has a chronic fear of enemies.

BIBLICAL PERSPECTIVE

The Word of God teaches us not to become bitter, hostile, or vengeful toward another person. If we do, we become the losers. We might not like what others do or say, but we must learn to love them as Christ commanded. Matthew 5 demonstrates how we are to act: to love those who hate us, rather than react in retaliation. We must recognize God as the answer to reconciliation and peace (Gal. 5:22, 23).

COUNSEL

Point out that not only must one ask for forgiveness for one's own attitude (e.g., of bitterness, resentment, hate), but also forgive one's enemy and ask that God forgive him.

Evaluate his feelings and attitudes toward the person. Are these feelings and attitudes Christlike? Pray for the fruit of the Spirit to increase in the counselee.

Suggest he go to the one with whom he has a difference to ask genuinely for forgiveness, and to seek ways to cultivate true friendship.

PRAYER

Dear Lord, thank you for your love and patience. I acknowledge that my feelings and attitudes have not been Christlike. I ask your forgiveness and the forgiveness of my friend. Give me a genuine love for my new friend. Thank you, Father, for also forgiving my friend for anything done or said against me. Thank you for giving me genuine love for my friend and showing me ways to cultivate it. In Jesus' name, amen.

REFERENCES

Psalm 23:5
God provides for needs

1 Corinthians 15:26
Death will be defeated

Matthew 5:43-48
Love your enemies

Psalm 18:47, 48
God is our avenger

Psalm 44:5-7
Victory through God

Proverbs 16:7
God causes enemies to be at peace with us

Philippians 4:13
Strength in Christ promised

Luke 23:34
Jesus forgave enemies

Acts 7:59, 60
Stephen forgave enemies

_____

_____

_____

_____

_____

_____

_____

_____

what good is that? Even the most wicked will lend to their own kind for full return!

Love your enemies! Do good to them! Lend to them! And don't be concerned about the fact that they won't repay. Then your reward from heaven will be very great, and you will truly be acting as sons of God: for he is kind to the unthankful and to those who are very wicked.

Try to show as much compassion as your Father does.

Never criticize or condemn—or it will all come back on you. Go easy on others, then they will do the same for you.

Romans 12:14, 19-21
If someone mistreats you because you are a Christian, don't curse him; pray that God will bless him.

Dear friends, never avenge yourselves. Leave that to God, for he has said that he will repay those who deserve it. [Don't take the law into your own hands.] Instead, feed your enemy if he is hungry. If he is thirsty give him something to drink and you will be "heaping coals of fire on his head." In other words, he will feel ashamed of himself for what he has done to you. Don't let evil get the upper hand but conquer evil by doing good.

SCRIPTURE

Proverbs 14:30
A relaxed attitude lengthens a man's life; jealousy rots it away.

1 Corinthians 3:3
For you are still only baby Christians, controlled by your own desires, not God's. When you are jealous of one another and divide up into quarreling groups, doesn't that prove you are still babies, wanting your own way? In fact, you are acting like people who don't belong to the Lord at all.

Galatians 5:19-21
But when you follow your own wrong inclinations your lives will produce these evil results: impure thoughts, eagerness for lustful pleasure, idolatry, spiritism (that is, encouraging the activity of demons), hatred and fighting, jealousy and anger, constant effort to get the best for yourself, complaints and criticisms, the feeling that everyone else is wrong except those in your own little group—and there will be wrong doctrine, envy, murder, drunkenness, wild parties, and all that sort of thing. Let me tell you again as I have before, that anyone living that sort of life will not inherit the Kingdom of God.

PROBLEM

Envy and jealousy are works of the flesh (Gal. 5:20) and a product of the natural sin of pride. Those who are envious or jealous may find themselves engaging in gossip, making snide remarks, and trying to build themselves up at the expense of others.

BIBLICAL PERSPECTIVE

Sin, when full-blown, produces destruction, tragedy, and death (Gal. 5:19-21; James 1:14, 15). So if one is envious or jealous, he may soon find himself beset with undesirable, destructive emotions. A judgmental attitude is often followed by hate. This leads to spiritual murder, character assassination, and other sins against those of whom one is envious or jealous.

COUNSEL

Salvation in Christ includes freedom from the bondage of sin (John 8:36). The baptism in the Holy Spirit can open the counselee's life to the abundance and gifts of God. The Holy Spirit produces the virtues and qualities of godliness in a Christian, leaving no place for sin (Gal. 5:22, 23).

The counselee has no reason to be envious. Remind him that, as a Christian, he is a King's kid, an heir to all that is Christ's. God has something better for him than he can imagine (1 Cor. 2:9).

Encourage the counselee to worship God in praise. Help him to focus his attention on God (Col. 3:1-4) rather than on his own lack, which leads to envy and jealousy. Affirm that, in Christ, love now prevails in his life and jealousy and envy are dead (1 Cor. 13:4). Affirm that honesty, not strife and envy, will allow him to walk in God's love and light (Rom. 13:13). And affirm that from this moment, he should seek to walk in the Spirit where there is no provoking of one another and no envy (Gal. 5:25, 26).

The counselee needs to rejoice and be glad when others are blessed or exalted. It pleases God and wins friends (Rom. 12:14-16).

PRAYER

Pray with the counselee for forgiveness of his envy/jealousy and that he might be filled with the Holy Spirit and know and experience the glory of God within him. Assist him in asking God to give him a vision of his glory and love and regard for those toward whom he (the counselee) has been envious and jealous. Help him pray for the fruit of the Spirit to be produced within him (Gal. 5:22, 23).

REFERENCES

1 Timothy 6:6
Money and possessions are left behind when we die

Proverbs 15:16
Treasure brings trouble

Philippians 4:11
Paul was happy whether he had much or little

Hebrews 13:5
Be satisfied with what you have

2 Corinthians 9:8
God will supply all your needs

FOLLOW-UP

Ask the counselee to list God's alternative behavior patterns for him and to begin practicing them. Encourage him to note all the praiseworthy things about those he was envious or jealous of. Then ask him to share those things with those people. The counselee will find a bond of love growing as he begins to see how God loves them.

James 3:14, 16
And by all means don't brag about being wise and good if you are bitter and jealous and selfish; that is the worst sort of lie. . . . For wherever there is jealousy or selfish ambition, there will be disorder and every other kind of evil.

John 10:10
The thief's purpose is to steal, kill, and destroy. My purpose is to give life in all its fullness.

SCRIPTURE

Leviticus 19:16
Don't gossip. Don't falsely accuse your neighbor of some crime, for I am Jehovah.

Psalm 19:14
May my spoken words and unspoken thoughts be pleasing even to you, O Lord my Rock and my Redeemer.

Proverbs 20:19
Don't tell your secrets to a gossip unless you want them broadcast to the world.

Matthew 7:12
Do for others what you want them to do for you. This is the teaching of the laws of Moses in a nutshell.

Matthew 18:15-17
If a brother sins against you, go to him privately and confront him with his fault. If he listens and confesses it, you have won back a brother. But if not, then take one or two others with you and go back to him again, proving everything you say by these witnesses. If he still refuses to listen, then take your case to the church, and if the church's verdict favors you, but he won't accept it, then the church should excommunicate him.

PROBLEM

Gossip is sharing private information, whether true or false, to those who are neither part of the problem nor the solution.

Someone has said, "Gossip is like mud thrown against a clean wall; it may not stick, but it leaves a mark."

BIBLICAL PERSPECTIVE

When we say things about others we would not say in their presence, we are disobeying God's Word (Lev. 19:16) and destroying that person's reputation. The Bible teaches that the sin of gossip is not merely the spreading of lies, but includes any form of interference in the personal affairs of others (2 Thess. 3:11; 1 Tim. 5:13).

COUNSEL

Gossip is a common sin among Christians because we find it so easy to justify. For example, we too often spread gossip packaged as "prayer requests."

Learn to recognize gossip. We should test a story before telling it; and we should critically evaluate the stories we hear from others. Is it true? Will the telling of this story benefit anyone? Will it bring glory to Christ? Would I want that story told about me, even if it was true?

Confess the sin of gossip. We have difficulty seeing this sin in our life. Therefore, we should earnestly pray, "Search me, O God, and know my heart; test my thoughts. Point out anything you find in me that makes you sad, and lead me along the path of everlasting life" (Ps. 139:23, 24).

Determine that you will never gossip again. At the beginning of each day offer this prayer: "May my spoken words and unspoken thoughts be pleasing even to you, O Lord my Rock and my Redeemer" (Ps. 19:14).

Throughout the day live by this principle: "And whatever you do or say, let it be as a representative of the Lord Jesus . . ." (Col. 3:17).

Encourage others every day. Become aware of those occasions which are prone to be gossipy, and transform them into opportunities for ministry.

"If a brother sins against you, go to him privately and confront him with his fault . . ." (Matt. 18:15).

"Encourage one another daily . . ." (Heb. 3:13, NIV).

"In response to all he has done for us, let us outdo each other in being helpful and kind to each other and in doing good" (Heb. 10:24).

"Encourage and warn each other, especially now that the day of his coming again is drawing near" (Heb. 10:25).

PRAYER

Encourage the counselee to pray and ask for God to forgive him for destroying others with gossip and to fill him with his Holy Spirit. Pray that the Holy Spirit will produce in him the fruit of the Spirit, self-control, and use him to encourage others.

REFERENCES

1 Corinthians 13
Love enables us to treat others right

Romans 1:28-32
Gossip and backbiting are terrible sins

Exodus 20:16
God commands us not to lie

2 Thessalonians 3:11, 12
Yet we hear that some of you are living in laziness, refusing to work, and wasting your time in gossiping. In the name of the Lord Jesus Christ we appeal to such people—we command them—to quiet down, get to work, and earn their own living.

James 3:2, 5, 6, 8
If anyone can control his tongue, it proves that he has perfect control over himself in every other way.

So also the tongue is a small thing, but what enormous damage it can do. A great forest can be set on fire by one tiny spark. And the tongue is a flame of fire. It is full of wickedness, and poisons every part of the body. And the tongue is set on fire by hell itself, and can turn our whole lives into a blazing flame of destruction and disaster.

But no human being can tame the tongue. It is always ready to pour out its deadly poison.

James 4:11
Don't criticize and speak evil about each other, dear brothers. If you do, you will be fighting against God's law of loving one another, declaring it is wrong. But your job is not to decide whether this law is right or wrong, but to obey it.

SCRIPTURE

Matthew 7:1, 2
Don't criticize, and then you won't be criticized. For others will treat you as you treat them.

John 8:7
They kept demanding an answer, so he stood up again and said, "All right, hurl the stones at her until she dies. But only he who never sinned may throw the first!"

Mark 11:25
But when you are praying, first forgive anyone you are holding a grudge against, so that your Father in heaven will forgive you your sins, too.

Luke 6:41
And why quibble about the speck in someone else's eye— his little fault—when a board is in your own?

Romans 14:4
They are God's servants, not yours. They are responsible to him, not to you. Let him tell them whether they are right or wrong. And God is able to make them do as they should.

PROBLEM

A judgmental/critical attitude stems from various sources: a strict, legalistic view of the Bible; an overbearing conscience; a tendency to be negative in thought, speech, and actions; and others. The problem may be seen as a manifestation of the common sin of pride.

BIBLICAL PERSPECTIVE

We should not even be judgmental of ourselves, let alone other people. The time for judgment will come, and it will be God who will judge us all (1 Cor. 4:3-5).

COUNSEL

The judgmental person must see the need to demonstrate forgiveness and mercy instead of criticism. Consider the story of Jesus and the woman caught in adultery (John 8:1-12).

We must look beyond a person's failings and try to see the "glory that is to be revealed" in him. If the person has not already accepted Jesus Christ as Savior, then pray for him to do so. If the person is saved, pray for the power of the Holy Spirit in forgiving that person and overlooking his faults.

Remind the counselee that, just as "God is not finished with me yet," he also is not finished with other persons.

PRAYER

In praying with the counselee, remind him to look at things with his spiritual eyes and to trust God to take care of a judging person's acts. Take a strong stand against any judgmental or critical attitude. Suggest asking for forgiveness when judgmental and critical feelings arise. Let him know that he can ask God to forgive the persons

who have annoyed him and that he also should
forgive them. Speak of God's peace and love and
emphasize that it is God, not we, who is to judge
others.

FOLLOW-UP
Suggest that the counselee find daily practical
ways to be of help to the person he has been
judging. A daily reading of Galatians 6:1-3 would
be helpful.

 Suggest to the counselee that he list all the
good qualities he can find in the person he has
been critical of. He should look for opportunities
to share that praise with the person.

SCRIPTURE

Matthew 5:38-40
The law of Moses says, "If a man gouges out another's eye, he must pay with his own eye. If a tooth gets knocked out, knock out the tooth of the one who did it." But I say: Don't resist violence! If you are slapped on one cheek, turn the other too. If you are ordered to court, and your shirt is taken from you, give your coat too.

Romans 12:17-21
Never pay back evil for evil. Do things in such a way that everyone can see you are honest clear through. Don't quarrel with anyone. Be at peace with everyone, just as much as possible. Dear friends, never avenge yourselves. Leave that to God, for he has said that he will repay those who deserve it. [Don't take the law into your own hands.] Instead, feed your enemy if he is hungry. If he is thirsty give him something to drink and you will be "heaping coals of fire on his head." In other words, he will feel ashamed of himself for what he has done to you.

PROBLEM

Vengeance is retaliation for an injury or offense. It springs from the natural and universal urge to get even with someone whom we believe has harmed us. (In some cultures, vengeance may be seen as a family duty. The family takes vengeance when a member's honor has been offended. This is true for some African, Oriental, and Latin American groups.)

BIBLICAL PERSPECTIVE

In the Old Testament the "eye for an eye and a tooth for a tooth" principle was not a ticket for revenge but a legal limit to prevent people from taking even further vengeance. The New Testament stresses that Christians, who have experienced the unmerited forgiveness and love of God, should not seek vengeance. Evil is to be overcome with good, forgiveness is to heal broken relationships, and enemies are to be loved. Such compassionate behavior follows the pattern of Christ and demonstrates to the world the newness of life in Christ (Matt. 5:38-48).

COUNSEL

Listen with an open mind to the person's complaint. Don't hastily say, "You shouldn't feel that way" or "What he did wasn't so bad after all, was it?" The counselee must feel you really understand his pain before he can trust you.

Ask the person if he is a Christian. If not, seek to lead the person to receive Jesus as Savior and Lord. He should ask for forgiveness and for newness of life. If the person is already saved, talk about his relationship with the Lord, perhaps referring to Romans 8:28 and making a statement like, "I believe if God has allowed this problem to come into your life he wants to bring something good out of it." Help assure the person that God can forgive his vindictive feelings and can overcome the desire for vengeance. Remind him that Christ set an example of love, patience, and forgiveness, even when dealing with his enemies.

Suggest that the person plan a specific action to encourage reconciliation and love. This might involve writing a letter, making an apology in person or by phone, or doing kindness in place of vengeance. In cases where the offense was between husband and wife, or between parent and child, you may want to refer to the sections of the handbook that deal with MARITAL RELATIONS and PARENT-CHILD RELATIONSHIPS. You may also want to refer the person to a local, Christ-centered pastor skilled in family and marital problems.

PRAYER
Lead the counselee in a prayer of forgiveness concerning the person who has offended him (Mark 11:25). Encourage him to make every effort to reconcile with the offender.

FOLLOW-UP
Suggest that the counselee make a list of people he has hated or not forgiven, then confess his sins and destroy the list. Christ died for those sins, and they are forgiven when confessed and repented of.

READING
The Renewed Mind by Larry Christenson

Ephesians 4:31–5:2
Stop being mean, bad-tempered and angry. Quarreling, harsh words, and dislike of others should have no place in your lives. Instead, be kind to each other, tenderhearted, forgiving one another, just as God has forgiven you because you belong to Christ.

REFERENCES

Matthew 18:21, 22
The necessity for forgiveness

Colossians 3:13
Forgive as God forgives

Luke 23:34
Jesus forgiving his executioners

Hebrews 10:30
Vengeance belongs to God

BONDAGE

SCRIPTURE

Psalm 119:104
*And since only your rules
can give me wisdom and
understanding, no wonder I
hate every false teaching.*

Mark 13:21-23
*And then if anyone tells you,
"This is the Messiah," or,
"That one is," don't pay any
attention. For there will be
many false Messiahs and
false prophets who will do
wonderful miracles that
would deceive, if possible,
even God's own children.
Take care! I have warned you!*

1 John 4:1-3
*Dearly loved friends, don't
always believe everything you
hear just because someone
says it is a message from
God: test it first to see if it
really is. For there are many
false teachers around, and
the way to find out if their
message is from the Holy
Spirit is to ask: Does it really
agree that Jesus Christ, God's
Son, actually became man
with a human body? If so,
then the message is from
God. If not, the message is
not from God but from one
who is against Christ, like
the "Antichrist" you have
heard about who is going to
come, and his attitude of
enmity against Christ is already abroad in the world.*

PROBLEM

A cult is any group whose beliefs directly oppose orthodox Christianity and who do not recognize Jesus Christ as the unique Son of God. Walter R. Martin in *The Kingdom of the Cults* states that a cult "is any religious group which differs significantly in one or more respects as to belief or practice, from those religious groups which are regarded as the normative expressions of religion in our total culture." A cult may be built around a personality figure or around a set of beliefs and interpretations. For example, Jehovah's Witnesses are, for the most part, followers of the interpretations of Charles T. Russell and J. F. Rutherford.

BIBLICAL PERSPECTIVE

There are many kinds and variations of religions in the world today. One group thinks it has the answer, while another group thinks it is right. We are to read the Word of God with a mind open to the Holy Spirit's teaching and search the Scriptures daily in order to ascertain the truth.

COUNSEL

The danger of a cult stems from deception. A person may believe false teaching if it makes him feel good or if he doesn't know any better. When someone knows the truth, he can recognize falsehood. Take the Scriptures at face value in all their simplicity. Search them in their entirety in order to judge whether a teaching is cultic, deviating from God's Word so as to pervert the clear teaching on important matters of faith and practice. These matters include teachings about God the Father, Jesus Christ, the Holy Spirit, salvation, sin, heaven, hell, Satan, baptism, and moral behavior.

Cults which pose as somehow Christian-oriented include the Unification Church ("Moonies"), the so-called "Children of God" headed by David "Moses" Berg, Jehovah's Witnesses, Mormonism, Christian Science, and The Way International. Beware also of cults which deceptively package Hinduism for the Western world such as the New Age movement, Transcendental Meditation, Rajneesh meditation centers, and many others.

If a person has been entangled with such a group, lead him to repent, renouncing any involvement. Explain to him the good news of salvation through faith in Jesus Christ. Then encourage him to participate in a local church fellowship which is Christ-centered and clearly teaches the Bible.

PRAYER
If the person cannot repent, pray for the person to understand the deception of the cult and to learn the truth about Jesus Christ. Look for the Spirit to reveal to you how to minister.

FOLLOW-UP
Read the following books on cults:

Kingdom of the Cults by Walter Martin
Larson's Book of Cults by Bob Larson
Mark of Cults by David Breese

Upon renouncing cultic beliefs and activities, a person must still make willful choices to change habits related to cultic activities. Old patterns, such as cult-oriented meditation, carried over into a new Christian life-style may cause difficulty and weaken the person's resistance to future satanic attacks.

2 Corinthians 11:13-15
God never sent those men at all; they are "phonies" who have fooled you into thinking they are Christ's apostles. Yet I am not surprised! Satan can change himself into an angel of light, so it is no wonder his servants can do it too, and seem like godly ministers. In the end they will get every bit of punishment their wicked deeds deserve.

REFERENCES

Galatians 1:8, 9
Warning about nongospel teaching

2 Corinthians 11:13-15
False apostles

Mark 13:21-23
False messiahs

2 Timothy 4:1-5
Admonition concerning false teaching

Deuteronomy 13:1-5; 18:20-22
Warning about false prophets and dreamers

Jeremiah 23
Destructiveness of unfaithful pastors

1 Peter 5:1-3
Elders to serve, not dictate

_____

_____

_____

_____

SCRIPTURE

John 8:31, 32, 36
Jesus said to them, "You are truly my disciples if you live as I tell you to, and you will know the truth, and the truth will set you free.

So if the Son sets you free, you will indeed be free."

Romans 7:21-25
It seems to be a fact of life that when I want to do what is right, I inevitably do what is wrong. I love to do God's will so far as my new nature is concerned; but there is something else deep within me, in my lower nature, that is at war with my mind and wins the fight and makes me a slave to the sin that is still within me. In my mind I want to be God's willing servant but instead I find myself still enslaved to sin.

So you see how it is: my new life tells me to do right, but the old nature that is still inside me loves to sin. Oh, what a terrible predicament I'm in! Who will free me from my slavery to this deadly lower nature? Thank God! It has been done by Jesus Christ our Lord. He has set me free.

PROBLEM

Many people, including Christians, are bound by the power of sin, various kinds of fear, legalism, and demonic influence. Jesus Christ is able to set us free from bondage—spiritual, emotional, and social.

BIBLICAL PERSPECTIVE

Jesus said that his purpose for coming to earth was to announce that captives shall be released and the downtrodden freed from their oppressors (Luke 4:18, 19). He also told his disciples that if they know the truth they will be free, and anyone set free by the Son will indeed be free (John 8:32, 36).

COUNSEL

Seek the Lord on behalf of the counselee, expecting discernment to be given to you by the Holy Spirit. If repentance from sin is needed, help the counselee deal with his sin. If demonic influence (oppression, possession) is discerned, exercise the authority that God has given you over Satan; believe that the counselee will be set free from his bondage. In order for the counselee to stay free from his bondage, help him recognize that when Jesus Christ died on the cross and arose from the grave, he made it possible for those who put their trust in him to be set free from every form of bondage. While we "wait anxiously for that day when God will give us our full rights as his children . . ." (Rom. 8:23), we can enjoy a measure of freedom the rest of the world cannot even imagine. Remember, we are the children of God. We are bound by the time, space, and physical limitations of this earth, but we can be delivered from the many bondages that we may be experiencing. Let's enjoy the freedom Christ paid for on Calvary.

Encourage the counselee to participate in a local church fellowship that is Christ-centered and clearly teaches the Bible. (See section on FREEDOM FROM DEMON BONDAGE.)

To be set free from	*Apply the principles of*
Loneliness	Ps. 23; John 14:15, 16, 18, 19
Fear of being with people	2 Tim. 1:7
Fear of telling others about Christ	Matt. 28:18-20; Acts 1:8; 2 Tim. 1:8
Fear of condemnation from God	John 5:24; Rom. 8:1, 2; 1 John 5:13
Wrong thoughts	Isa. 26:3; Phil. 4:8, 9; Col. 3:15, 16
Sinful habits	Rom. 7:21-25; 1 Cor. 10:13; 2 Tim. 2:22
Doubts about the effectiveness of prayer	Luke 11:1-4; James 1:5-8; James 5:13-18; 1 John 5:14, 15
Pressures to copy the customs of this world	Rom. 12:1, 2
Fear of death	Ps. 23:4; 1 Cor. 15:54-57; 2 Cor. 5:8, 9
Financial bondage	Mal. 3:8-12; Prov. 22:7; Matt. 6:31-34; Phil. 4:18-20
Demonic oppression	John 8:32, 38; James 4:7; 1 Pet. 5:8, 9; Eph. 6:10-18
The legalistic expectations of others	Rom. 14; 1 Cor. 8; Col. 2:16; 1 Tim. 4:1-5

PRAYER

Pray that Christ will set the counselee free, far beyond his expectations, as he studies and applies the principles of God's Word. Pray that he will have a ministry to those who are still bound.

Romans 8:33, 34
Who dares accuse us whom God has chosen for his own? Will God? No! He is the one who has forgiven us and given us right standing with himself. Who then will condemn us? Will Christ? No! For he is the one who died for us and came back to life again for us and is sitting at the place of highest honor next to God, pleading for us there in heaven.

1 John 5:12-15
So whoever has God's Son has life; whoever does not have his Son, does not have life. I have written this to you who believe in the Son of God so that you may know you have eternal life. And we are sure of this, that he will listen to us whenever we ask him for anything in line with his will. And if we really know he is listening when we talk to him and make our requests, then we can be sure that he will answer us.

SCRIPTURE

Deuteronomy 18:10-13
For example, any Israeli who presents his child to be burned to death as a sacrifice to heathen gods, must be killed. No Israeli may practice black magic, or call on the evil spirits for aid, or be a fortune teller, or be a serpent charmer, medium, or wizard, or call forth the spirits of the dead. Anyone doing these things is an object of horror and disgust to the Lord, and it is because the nations do these things that the Lord your God will displace them. You must walk blamelessly before the Lord your God.

Ephesians 6:12
For we are not fighting against people made of flesh and blood, but against persons without bodies—the evil rulers of the unseen world, those mighty satanic beings and great evil princes of darkness who rule this world; and against huge numbers of wicked spirits in the spirit world.

Matthew 8:28, 32
. . . two men with demons in them met him. They lived in a cemetery and were so dangerous that no one could go through that area. . . . "All right," Jesus told them. "Begone." And they came out of the men and entered the pigs, and the whole herd rushed over a cliff and drowned in the water below.

PROBLEM

Demon bondage can be brought about when an individual is possessed, oppressed, or is in rebellion toward God (sins of the flesh). It takes God's discernment to determine which of these is producing the bondage in an individual's life.

BIBLICAL PERSPECTIVE

The Bible makes it clear that there are demons, or evil spirits, in the world that interfere in people's lives (Eph. 6:11-19). Evil forces or powers influence or control the minds of individuals, bring sickness, and cause undesirable behavior, inability to function normally, and even suicide. As a result of these forces, people can become a danger to themselves as well as others.

COUNSEL

Anyone can be assured of victory over demons if he has received Jesus as Savior and Lord (John 1:12), and has received the baptism in the Holy Spirit (Acts 1:8). The Holy Spirit guides us into truth, empowers us, and intercedes for us. He also gives us spiritual gifts, such as discerning of spirits, for our welfare and that of others (1 Cor. 12; Mark 16:9-20).

Demonic influences may show themselves in a number of ways. Determine from which of the following specific areas the counselee may need to be delivered:

1. Compulsion to abuse animals or people.
2. Sexual perversion and immorality (homosexuality, molestation, etc.).
3. A compulsion to abuse his body (drugs, alcohol, gluttony, abuse or misuse of other substances etc.).
4. A seeking of spiritual knowledge through Eastern religions and other counterfeit reli-

gious groups (TM, yoga, humanism, etc.).

5. Involvement in occult practices (fortune-telling, satanism, etc.).
6. Mental distress or oppression (anxiety, fear, anger, disorientation, etc.).
7. Psychological disorders (split and multiple personalities, paranoia, etc.).
8. Unusual physical disorders that may be caused by demons (Matt. 9:32, 33).
9. Lack of freedom or joy in the Lord (spiritual bondage).
10. Inability or constant refusal to repent of sin, though he knows he is sinning (rebellion).

(See Bible passages under "References" and look in a Bible dictionary and concordance for examples of the above.)

Show the counselee that Jesus came to free those under demon bondage. "Anyone who calls upon the name of the Lord will be saved" (Rom. 10:13). The terms *saved* and *salvation* include a person's spiritual, physical, and mental health.

The counselee must be led to pray sincerely to the Lord for forgiveness of sin. Advise him that the Lord will forgive him, cleanse him, be his Savior and Lord and baptize (fill) him with the Holy Spirit (1 John 1:8, 9; John 1:12; Luke 11:13; Acts 1:8). The Holy Spirit will give him the power to overcome demon bondage, activity, and influence. He can be free. The counselee can experience an abundant, full, meaningful life with the joy and purpose God desires for him (John 10:10).

The counselee needs to be sure his problem is not a fleshly, willful one on his part. Help him to take a bold, fearless inventory of himself. He must choose whom he will serve: self and fleshly desires—Satan—or God? Encourage him to repent of all sinful desires. Help him renounce sin

Acts 5:16
And crowds came in from the Jerusalem suburbs, bringing their sick folk and those possessed by demons; and every one of them was healed.

Galatians 5:19-21
But when you follow your own wrong inclinations your lives will produce these evil results: impure thoughts, eagerness for lustful pleasure, idolatry, spiritism (that is, encouraging the activity of demons), hatred and fighting, jealousy and anger, constant effort to get the best for yourself, complaints and criticisms, the feeling that everyone else is wrong except those in your own little group—and there will be wrong doctrine, envy, murder, drunkenness, wild parties, and all that sort of thing. Let me tell you again as I have before, that anyone living that sort of life will not inherit the Kingdom of God.

REFERENCES

1 Samuel 28
King Saul consults a medium
and is paralyzed with fright

Matthew 8:28-32; 9:32, 33;
12:43-45; 15:22, 28;
17:15-18
Jesus casts out demons

Mark 1:23-27
Jesus silences a demon

Luke 8:2; 10:17
Mary Magdalene, possessed
by seven demons, is delivered by Jesus

Acts 5:16; 8:7; 19:12
Christ's followers cast out
demons

READING

Defeated Enemies by Corrie
ten Boom
Demons in the World Today
by Merrill Unger
The Devil's Alphabet by Kurt
Koch
His Infernal Majesty by
Dave Breese
Demons by Lester Sumrall

———————————
———————————
———————————
———————————
———————————
———————————
———————————
———————————

and sinfulness and its ingrained habits. Then advise him to commit himself to Christ with determination and resolve. After the counselee has done this, assure him, on the foundation of Scripture, that he is a child of God and has been forgiven.

One cannot reckon an evil spirit dead, crucify an evil agent, or even cast out the flesh. The counselee must crucify the flesh (Gal. 2:20) and its desires and cast out evil spirits (James 4:7). And when demons or evil spirits are cast out, the counselee needs something to replace them, lest they return (Matt. 12:43-48).

As the counselee receives God's nature, the traits of his fleshly nature (such as irresponsible behavior, pride, and lack of love) will be replaced by the fruit of the Spirit (Gal. 5:22, 23).

His greatest need is to continually study God's Word. Encourage him to meditate upon the Bible day and night (Josh. 1:8) to put on the whole armor of God that he might be able to effectively overcome the forces of evil (Eph. 6:10-18). Jesus answered Satan with the Word of God (Luke 4:1-13). The counselee can do the same. He needs to pray without ceasing (1 Thess. 5:17); also direct the counselee to a Christ-centered pastor, counselor, or church group that clearly teaches the Bible. (See section on DELIVER-ANCE.)

PRAYER

Assist the counselee in honoring God with thanksgiving and praise. As he gives God first place in his thoughts and actions, Satan and his demons will find there's no room in that life for them.

PROBLEM

The occult includes such diverse phenomena as precognition (fortune telling), ESP, telepathy, clairvoyance, automatic writing, ouija boards, astrology, tea leaf reading, palmistry, mind expansion, drug use, hypnotism, mind control, transcendental meditation, yoga, sorcery (witchcraft), telekinesis, levitation, astral projection, spiritualism, seances, satanism, and others.

Throughout history we see numerous examples of diminishing spiritual life leading to legalism, to materialism, to seeking life's answers outside God's Word, and to involvement with the occult, which often involves drug use, idolatry, and sexual perversions.

BIBLICAL PERSPECTIVE

Though there are many forms of satanic influence in the world, we have the absolute authority, through the power of Christ, to bind the powers of darkness and dispel them. They must do our bidding as we speak in the name of Jesus (Luke 10:17-19; Eph. 1:17-23; Mark 16:17; Matt. 16:19; 18:18).

COUNSEL

Occult activity must be renounced verbally.

Determine if the person is willing to repent and lead him to repentance. If he is not, pray for deliverance. The power of the Holy Spirit is needed for a victorious life that has no place for occult practices.

Most counselees who mention occult involvement have probably been reading occult literature and having fellowship with others practicing occultism. These must be replaced by Scripture reading and by fellowship with strong, growing Christians. Emphasize that a complete break with occultism is necessary. Refer the person to

SCRIPTURE

Exodus 22:18
A sorceress shall be put to death.

Deuteronomy 18:10-13
For example, any Israeli who presents his child to be burned to death as a sacrifice to heathen gods, must be killed. No Israeli may practice black magic, or call on the evil spirits for aid, or be a fortune teller, or be a serpent charmer, medium, or wizard, or call forth the spirits of the dead. Anyone doing these things is an object of horror and disgust to the Lord, and it is because the nations do these things that the Lord your God will displace them. You must walk blamelessly before the Lord your God.

Revelation 21:8
But cowards who turn back from following me, and those who are unfaithful to me, and the corrupt, and murderers, and the immoral, and those conversing with demons, and idol worshipers and all liars—their doom is in the Lake that burns with fire and sulphur. This is the Second Death.

_____

_____

_____

_____

_____

Galatians 5:19-21
But when you follow your own wrong inclinations your lives will produce these evil results: impure thoughts, eagerness for lustful pleasure, idolatry, spiritism (that is, encouraging the activity of demons), hatred and fighting, jealousy and anger, constant effort to get the best for yourself, complaints and criticisms, the feeling that everyone else is wrong except those in your own little group—and there will be wrong doctrine, envy, murder, drunkenness, wild parties, and all that sort of thing. Let me tell you again as I have before, that anyone living that sort of life will not inherit the Kingdom of God.

Luke 4:18, 19
The Spirit of the Lord is upon me; he has appointed me to preach Good News to the poor; he has sent me to heal the brokenhearted and to announce that captives shall be released and the blind shall see, that the downtrodden shall be freed from their oppressors, and that God is ready to give blessings to all who come to him.

a Christ-centered church that clearly teaches the Bible, preferably where there has been experience in dealing with occultism.

PRAYER
Lead the counselee in a prayer such as this: Father, in the name of Jesus I come, realizing you are a jealous God and will have no other gods before you. I repent of the sins of the occult and ask your forgiveness. Forgive me for all my sins. I give myself to you and turn my back on Satan and his works. Be my Lord and Savior. Amen.

FOLLOW-UP
The counselee should saturate himself with the Scriptures, beginning with the Gospel of John and continuing with the rest of the New Testament. He should acquire a Bible study guide and get involved with a Spirit-led fellowship. When the person knows the real God, he will recognize all counterfeits.

READING
Defeated Enemies by Corrie ten Boom
Demons in the World Today by Merrill Unger

_____

_____

_____

_____

_____

PROBLEM

Shepherdship is dictatorship in which a person who perceives himself as an immature Christian submits himself completely to the leading of an "elder." The elders (shepherds) are appointed in much the same way as in other hierarchies, with one submitting to the next higher in a chain of command. Total discipline is imposed on those who submit themselves to an elder. Tithes and offerings are given to the elder, and his leadership is total, even extending over the person's family life. Failure to obey the shepherd can lead to verbal condemnation or being cast out of the fellowship.

There are positive aspects of this system: the Word is taught; the system is built around the gospel; many people are ministered to by the elders. But the most significant aspect of the shepherding system is that one person submits his will completely to another individual, the shepherd or elder.

BIBLICAL PERSPECTIVE

The Lord alone is our shepherd, and no other shepherd or leader can be our Lord. The Bible indicates that we are to submit ourselves to one another, (Rom. 12:10) but this does not require that one person dominate another's will. We may go to our pastor or other respected leader to question him about important decisions in our lives, but even after hearing that leader's counsel we must still make our own decisions. It is an evasion of responsibility when we allow others to make important decisions for us and then, if the consequences are bad, claim that "my shepherd made me do it" (Rom. 14:12; Mark 10:42-45). With good reason we seek the advice of mature Christians, but we ourselves are to be responsible and give account of our actions to God.

SCRIPTURE

John 10:4, 5, 27
He walks ahead of them; and they follow him, for they recognize his voice. They won't follow a stranger but will run from him, for they don't recognize his voice.

My sheep recognize my voice, and I know them, and they follow me.

Galatians 5:13
For, dear brothers, you have been given freedom: not freedom to do wrong, but freedom to love and serve each other.

Luke 22:25-27
Jesus told them, "In this world the kings and great men order their slaves around, and the slaves have no choice but to like it! But among you, the one who serves you best will be your leader. Out in the world the master sits at the table and is served by his servants. But not here! For I am your servant."

Mark 10:42-45
So Jesus called them to him and said, "As you know, the kings and great men of the earth lord it over the people: but among you it is different. Whoever wants to be great among you must be your servant. And whoever wants to be greatest of all must be the slave of all. For even I, the Messiah, am not here to be served, but to help others, and to give my life as a ransom for many."

Romans 14:12
Yes, each of us will give an account of himself to God.

_____

_____

_____

_____

_____

_____

_____

_____

_____

_____

_____

_____

_____

_____

_____

_____

_____

_____

_____

_____

_____

_____

_____

_____

COUNSEL

There is a vast difference between seeking wise counsel from mature Christians and being told what to do by a shepherd or group of shepherds. We should allow no person to dictate to us how to live our lives, even if we respect that person's judgment. Regrettably, many persons who have submitted themselves to shepherds have allowed themselves to be told whom to marry, whether to divorce or stay married, where to work, whether to visit relatives, and so on. Submission can become total obedience to a person.

The counselee needs to be reminded that, like Jesus, our total obedience is given to God alone. And Jesus alone is our only mediator, the one bridge between God and us. Though the church is enriched by the work of prophets, teachers, pastors, evangelists, and apostles, no other human being is necessary to bring us into contact with God and his guidance. Jesus stated that his sheep—both mature Christians and those less mature—hear his voice.

The counselee has probably been attracted to the biblically-based teaching and morals of the Shepherdship proponents. However, our desire to live a godly life does not necessarily mean we must submit ourselves to the bondage of a hierarchical system or an elder of that system. True shepherds strive, like Jesus, to serve, not to dominate. The counselee is probably capable of discerning whether his pastor or elder is genuinely working to serve others or to be served by others. He may need to be reminded that there are many mature Christians who are able to provide guidance without insisting that their advice be accepted as law.

PRAYER

Pray that the Holy Spirit will guide the person into all truth, according to Jesus' word in John 14:26 and 16:13. Pray that the person's bondage may be broken and that no bitterness toward the elder(s) may remain. Pray for the elders, that they might see the error of the shepherding system. Pray for unity in the church, so that Christ, not any appointed leaders, might have the preeminence in all things.

REFERENCES

2 Corinthians 3:17
The Spirit gives freedom

Galatians 2:4
No bondage to others

Romans 6:16
Choosing our own master

Psalm 23
The true Shepherd

FOLLOW-UP

The counselee should seek out a Christ-centered church fellowship that clearly teaches the Bible and study passages (especially the Gospel of John) that speak of Christ's lordship and the need for Christians to minister to one another.

READING

Discipleship, the Jesus View by Bill Ligon

SCRIPTURE

Psalm 119:11
I have thought much about your words, and stored them in my heart so that they would hold me back from sin.

Matthew 6:13
Don't bring us into temptation, but deliver us from the Evil One. Amen.

Matthew 26:41
Keep alert and pray. Otherwise temptation will overpower you. For the spirit indeed is willing, but how weak the body is!

1 Corinthians 10:13
But remember this—the wrong desires that come into your life aren't anything new and different. Many others have faced exactly the same problems before you. And no temptation is irresistible. You can trust God to keep the temptation from becoming so strong that you can't stand up against it, for he has promised this and will do what he says. He will show you how to escape temptation's power so that you can bear up patiently against it.

2 Timothy 2:2
For you must teach others those things you and many others have heard me speak about. Teach these great truths to trustworthy men who will, in turn, pass them on to others.

PROBLEM

All of us have wrong desires and feel an inner, urge to disobey God's commands. Each day we are tempted and choose between right and wrong.

BIBLICAL PERSPECTIVE

While everyone of us is tempted to sin, no temptation is irresistible; God is able to keep it from becoming too strong, and will show us how to escape temptation's power (1 Cor. 10:13).

COUNSEL

Understand how Satan tempts us (based on Luke 4 and other Scriptures).

- Temptation often comes when we are alone and makes us feel all alone (4:1, 2).
- Satan tries to make us doubt the validity and reject the authority of God's Word (Luke 3:22; Gen. 3:1-5).
- Satan promises to satisfy our natural, legitimate appetites in the wrong way (4:3).
- Satan shows us how we can fulfill noble ambitions and reach worthy goals by the wrong methods (4:5-7).
- Temptation falsely promises immediate satisfaction (4:6, 7).
- Satan's goal is our destruction (4:9).
- Temptation uses the spectacular to feed our spiritual pride (4:9-11).
- Satan thrives on the misuse of Scripture (4:10, 11).
- Temptation is not constant, but it will return in full strength when we are weak (4:13).

Learn how to overcome the power of temptation (based on Luke 4 and other Scriptures).

- Know that you are a child of God (Luke 3:22; 2 Pet. 1:10).
- Be filled with the Holy Spirit (4:1; Eph. 5:18).
- Obey the Holy Spirit, and you won't always be doing the things your evil nature wants you to (4:1; Gal. 5:16).
- Memorize the Scriptures so you will be able to quote God's Word when tempted (Ps. 119:11; Luke 4:4, 8, 12; Eph. 6:17).
- Run away from anything that gives you evil thoughts (2 Tim. 2:22).
- Give yourself humbly to God and resist the devil (James 4:7).

Obviously, all of this counsel is for the Christian, because as Jesus said, "Apart from me you can't do a thing" (John 15:5). It is impossible to resist temptation without the power of God, and praise the Lord, Jesus can set us free from the terrible predicaments temptation causes (Rom. 7:25).

PRAYER
Pray that the counselee will learn to rely on the power of the Holy Spirit in him and will lean on the Word of God to resist temptation.

FOLLOW-UP
Study the Scriptures referred to in this chapter and the following examples of those who resisted temptation.

Abraham—Genesis 14:17-24
Joseph—Genesis 39
Elisha—2 Kings 5:16
Job—Job 2:9, 10
Daniel—Daniel 1:8
Daniel's friends—Daniel 3
Peter—Acts 8:14-23

James 4:7
So give yourselves humbly to God. Resist the devil and he will flee from you.

SCRIPTURE

Matthew 12:31, 32
Even blasphemy against me or any other sin, can be forgiven—all except one; speaking against the Holy Spirit shall never be forgiven, either in this world or in the world to come.

Mark 3:28-30
*"I solemnly declare that any sin of man can be forgiven, even blasphemy against me; but blasphemy against the Holy Spirit can never be forgiven. It is an eternal sin."
He told them this because they were saying he did his miracles by Satan's power (instead of acknowledging it was by the Holy Spirit's power).*

John 10:37, 38
Don't believe me unless I do miracles of God. But if I do, believe them even if you don't believe me. Then you will become convinced that the Father is in me, and I in the Father.

_____

_____

_____

_____

_____

_____

_____

_____

PROBLEM

Many persons express the fear that they have committed the unpardonable sin and that God will never forgive them. While the unpardonable sin refers, in traditional Christian teaching, to the total and persistent denial of the presence of God in Christ, many persons are not fully aware of this meaning and are consumed with guilt because they assume (often wrongly) that they have committed the sin.

BIBLICAL PERSPECTIVE

Christian teaching about the unpardonable sin stems from remarks in the Gospels about the casting out of demons. Jesus' opponents implied that the practice of exorcism showed that Jesus was somehow in league with Satan. Jesus flatly denied this, saying that his power came from the Spirit of God. His words are a warning against attributing the good things of God to the power of Satan. To reject Jesus' miracles is to reject and spurn the divine presence in the world. Matthew 12:24, 31, 32 (and parallel passages in Luke and Mark) show that Jesus considered it unforgivable to speak blasphemy against the Holy Spirit (that is, by denying the Spirit's power or ascribing it to demonic forces).

The unpardonable sin is not a single rash act (as many guilt-ridden people seem to think), but rather the deliberate and persistent rejection of Christ and his divine work. To encounter Christ and his work and to reject him is to condemn oneself to utter loss. In a sense, the warning against the unpardonable sin is a warning of how important it is to accept Christ and the salvation he offers us. Paul had been a blasphemer and persecutor of Christ. No doubt he, like most of the Pharisees, believed that the works of Christ were not the work of God. But Paul told Timothy that what he had done or said was not the conscious, willful act of blasphemy of which Jesus spoke. In other words, in spite of Paul's early hostility toward Christ and Christians, he was not guilty of the unpardonable sin. Words and deeds against Christ do not mean that the person can never receive forgiveness, for Paul did, and so have many others.

COUNSEL

The counselee may be agonizing over having committed the unpardonable sin. Many Christians really have only a vague idea of what the unpardonable sin is, so you may want to spend some time talking through the Scriptures above and clarifying the nature of blasphemy. This alone may put the person's mind at ease, since he may have held a completely wrong view of the unpardonable sin.

You may be dealing with a person who feels he has thoughtlessly, in some rash moment, spoken harsh (and unforgivable) words against God. This person needs assurance that the unpardonable sin is a more deliberate, conscious, continued rejection of God and his power. Few Christians are likely to commit such a sin, though in severe stress they may speak angry words against God. But God is willing to forgive such sins. They are not of eternal consequence.

Any person who is anxious over having committed the unpardonable sin almost surely never committed it. A person who is a genuine blasphemer would feel no need for repentance. We have the assurance that God will never reject a truly contrite person, so we can feel certain that a repentant counselee has not committed real blasphemy.

1 Timothy 1:12, 13
How thankful I am to Christ Jesus our Lord for choosing me as one of his messengers, and giving me the strength to be faithful to him, even though I used to scoff at the name of Christ. I hunted down his people, harming them in every way I could. But God had mercy on me because I didn't know what I was doing, for I didn't know Christ at that time.

REFERENCES

Proverbs 3:5, 6
Trusting God completely

1 John 1:9
Sin confessed is forgiven

Matthew 10:25
Expect the same as your
teacher receives

1 Corinthians 12:3
The Spirit-led cannot curse
Jesus

Ephesians 4:30
God's mark of ownership

1 John 5:6-10
Importance of affirming
Christ as the Son of God

READING

Grace Abounding by John
Bunyan

_____

_____

_____

_____

_____

_____

_____

God's grace is sufficient to calm the troubled person. The person needs to be assured that, though the unpardonable sin does have eternal consequences, all other sins may be forgiven.

It is helpful to remember that fear of having committed the unpardonable sin is a weapon used by Satan. Such great men as Martin Luther and John Bunyan feared at times that they had committed the sin and were thus forever cut off from God. Satan seeks to destroy our relationship with God by leading us to think that we ourselves have caused the relationship to end. He would rather see us wallowing in guilt and despair than enjoying fellowship with a forgiving God. But we can be victorious over such deceptions of the devil.

PRAYER

Lead the counselee in a prayer of repentance and faith. Thank God for the revelation that this sin was not committed. Pray that the counselee will receive God's peace and recommit himself to the Lord Jesus.

In the case of the person who feels he is bombarded with the temptation to commit the unpardonable sin, pray that he will triumph over the temptation and that all demonic influences in his life will be cast out.

CHURCH

SCRIPTURE

Matthew 28:18, 19
He told his disciples, "I have been given all authority in heaven and earth. Therefore go and make disciples in all the nations, baptizing them into the name of the Father and of the Son and of the Holy Spirit."

Romans 6:4, 5
Your old sin-loving nature was buried with him by baptism when he died, and when God the Father, with glorious power, brought him back to life again, you were given his wonderful new life to enjoy. For you have become a part of him, and so you died with him, so to speak, when he died; and now you share his new life, and shall rise as he did.

2 Corinthians 5:17
When someone becomes a Christian he becomes a brand new person inside. He is not the same any more. A new life has begun!

Ephesians 2:8, 9
Because of his kindness you have been saved through trusting Christ. And even trusting is not of yourselves, it too is a gift from God. Salvation is not a reward for the good we have done, so none of us can take any credit for it.

PROBLEM

The ordinance of water baptism is an important teaching of Scripture and practice of the church. But many are confused about its place in the Christian's life, which method should be practiced, and its essential meaning.

BIBLICAL PERSPECTIVE

Jesus told his disciples to make disciples of all nations and baptize those who put their trust in him (Matt. 28:18, 19). And Paul explained that baptism symbolizes our identification with the death, burial, and resurrection of Christ (Rom. 6:2-5).

COUNSEL

Water baptism is only for those who have first put their trust in Christ as Savior. A study of the New Testament will illustrate the point: those who believed on the Day of Pentecost (Acts 2:41); when Philip preached at Samaria (Acts 8:12); the treasurer of Ethiopia in the Gaza Desert (Acts 8:26-39); and others.

To understand the importance of water baptism in the life of the Christian today, we need to examine:

The Mandate of Baptism. Jesus commanded it (Matt. 28:18, 19). While Scripture makes it clear that baptism is not optional, it must also be understood that salvation is not in any way dependent on baptism (Eph. 2:8, 9).

The Method of Baptism. The method of baptism seems to be implied in the Greek word *baptismos,* which is not literally translated in most English versions of the New Testament, but transliterated. The Greek lexicons give the definition of *baptismos* as "dip, immerse, submerge." The early church understood this and used the Latin word *mersio,* which means to immerse.

The Meaning of Baptism. In Romans 6:1-11 Paul pointed to baptism as an object lesson, enabling his readers to more clearly understand what happened to them personally when Christ was crucified, buried, and brought back to life again. The meaning of baptism is summarized in verse 4: "Your old sin-loving nature was buried with him by baptism when he died, and when God the Father, with glorious power, brought him back to life again, you were given his wonderful new life to enjoy." In baptism, the Christian identifies himself with the living Christ.

Anyone who has put his trust in Christ as Savior and is living the Christian life should be water baptized. Being baptized will not make him any more a Christian, but it will be a public testimony that he has committed himself to a life of following Christ.

PRAYER

Pray that this beautiful object lesson, water baptism, will be more meaningful than ever before. Pray that if the one you are counseling decides to be baptized, he will be the living testimony unbelievers need to see, and that they will trust in Christ because of his baptismal service.

FOLLOW-UP

Study the Scriptures that have been quoted or mentioned in this chapter. Not all Christian churches offer baptism in the same way. Some sprinkle water on the head and others pour water over the head. Immersion in a body of water is the type of baptism that comes closest to that of the biblical command. Focus your attention on the beauty of this truth, and not so much on the controversy over which method of baptism should be practiced. Remember what the Lord said to Samuel: "Men judge by outward appearance, but I look at a man's thoughts and intentions" (1 Sam. 16:7).

Colossians 2:11, 12
When you came to Christ he set you free from your evil desires, not by a bodily operation of circumcision but by a spiritual operation, the baptism of your souls. For in baptism you see how your old, evil nature died with him and was buried with him; and then you came up out of death with him into a new life because you trusted the Word of the mighty God who raised Christ from the dead.

SCRIPTURE

Acts 2:40-47
Then Peter preached a long sermon, telling about Jesus and strongly urging all his listeners to save themselves from the evils of their nation. And those who believed Peter were baptized—about 3,000 in all! They joined with the other believers in regular attendance at the apostles' teaching sessions and at the Communion services and prayer meetings.

A deep sense of awe was on them all, and the apostles did many miracles.

And all the believers met together constantly and shared everything with each other, selling their possessions and dividing with those in need. They worshiped together regularly at the Temple each day, met in small groups in homes for Communion, and shared their meals with great joy and thankfulness, praising God. The whole city was favorable to them, and each day God added to them all who were being saved.

Ephesians 5:25
And you husbands, show the same kind of love to your wives as Christ showed to the church when he died for her.

PROBLEM

There are three common questions people ask about the church: Is it really necessary to attend church? What is a church? Which church should I attend?

BIBLICAL PERSPECTIVE

The church is so important that Christ died for it (Eph. 5:25). And Christians are instructed by Scripture not to neglect church meetings (Heb. 10:25).

COUNSEL

Is it really necessary to attend church? To understand why church attendance is so important, it is necessary to know the meaning of *church.* We often think of a church as a building, but the New Testament Greek word *ekklesia,* which is translated "church," means an assembly of people. Literally, ekklesia means "the called-out-ones." So when the writer of Hebrews 10:25 urges Christians not to neglect their church meetings, he is not stressing the importance of a church building, but the frequent gathering of Christians for worship, fellowship, and study of God's Word.

Going to church will not save you, but if you are a Christian, you need to attend church for your own spiritual growth and the encouragement of others.

What church should I attend? That question cannot be answered by a denominational name, style of worship, or list of weekly activities. You need to find a church where:

Worship permeates every activity. "May he [God] be given glory forever and ever through endless ages because of his master plan of salvation for the Church through Jesus Christ" (Eph. 3:21). Jesus said that "where two or three gather together because they are mine, I will be right there among them." So it must be that when Christians gather at church, they should experience a little bit of heaven, because Jesus is there. In heaven the angels sing: "The Lamb is worthy . . . the Lamb who was slain. He is worthy to receive the power, and the riches, and the wisdom, and the strength, and the honor, and the glory, and the blessing" (Rev. 5:12). Attend a church where the people enjoy worshiping the Lord. And that can be done in a variety of styles.

The Word of God is taught accurately and clearly. "Faith comes from listening to this Good News—the Good News about Christ" (Rom. 10:17). If you attend a church where the Bible is faithfully taught, you will find it easier to follow Paul's instruction: "Know what his Word says and means" (2 Tim. 2:15). And you will "grow in spiritual strength and become better acquainted with our Lord and Savior Jesus Christ . . ." (2 Pet. 3:18). Attend a church where you will hear God's voice above all the other voices.

Fellowship is sweet among the Christians. Fellowship is more than having dinner together. It is a close bond between Christians that results in helpfulness, kindness, doing good, and encouragement (Heb. 10:24, 25). Attend a Christ-centered church that clearly teaches the Bible where you can enjoy rich fellowship, not merely superficial relationships.

· *Service is performed in love and in the name of Christ.* Christian service may take many forms (singing, teaching, witnessing, helping the poor, etc.), but it is only pleasing to the Lord when it is the direct result of worship. In fact, worship and service are inseparable; every task should be done as worship unto the Lord. "Remember what Christ taught and let his words enrich your

Hebrews 10:24, 25
In response to all he has done for us, let us outdo each other in being helpful and kind to each other and in doing good.
Let us not neglect our church meetings, as some people do, but encourage and warn each other, especially now that the day of his coming back again is drawing near.

REFERENCES

John 15
Live in Christ, and let Christ live in you

1 Corinthians 12
Each Christian is an important part of the body of Christ, the Church

1 Corinthians 13
The most excellent way to serve in the church is by demonstrating love

_____

_____

_____

_____

_____

_____

_____

_____

_____

_____

_____

_____

_____

_____

_____

lives and make you wise; teach them to each other and sing them out in psalms and hymns and spiritual songs, singing to the Lord with thankful hearts. And whatever you do or say, let it be a representative of the Lord Jesus, and come with him into the presence of God the Father to give him your thanks" (Col. 3:16, 17). Attend a church where service unto the Lord is more than a Sunday affair.

Is church membership important? Acts 2:40-47 describes the growth and activities of the early church. Verse 47 says that "each day God added to them all who were being saved." That clearly shows that all who are saved are part of the church. So joining the local church is not a requirement for salvation, but a way you can publicly announce that you are a member of God's family. However, from a very practical standpoint, the establishment of a membership role enables church leaders to know who they can count on. Consider church membership a commitment to Christ and other Christians, and be sure the church leaders really can count on you.

PRAYER
Pray that the Holy Spirit will examine and purify the counselees' motives for joining a local church, and that he will lead them to make a wise choice—one which will result in their spiritual growth, the encouragement of others, and glorifying God.

GOD'S COMMANDS

SCRIPTURE

John 8:31
Jesus said to them, "You are truly my disciples if you live as I tell you to."

Luke 9:23
Then he said to all, "Anyone who wants to follow me must put aside his own desires and conveniences and carry his cross with him every day and keep close to me!"

Acts 1:8
But when the Holy Spirit has come upon you, you will receive power to testify about me with great effect, to the people in Jerusalem, throughout Judea, in Samaria, and to the ends of the earth, about my death and resurrection.

Matthew 28:18-20
He told his disciples, "I have been given all authority in heaven and earth. Therefore go and make disciples in all the nations, baptizing them into the name of the Father and of the Son and of the Holy Spirit, and then teach these new disciples to obey all the commands I have given you; and be sure of this—that I am with you always, even to the end of the world."

PROBLEM

Once a person has put his trust in Christ he is a Christian. But unless he is filled with the Spirit and learns to eat solid spiritual food, he will always be a baby Christian, controlled by his own desires and not God's (1 Cor. 3:1).

BIBLICAL PERSPECTIVE

Jesus told his disciples they were to go and make disciples in all the nations, and then teach these new disciples to obey all the commands he had given them (Matt. 28:19, 20).

And just as Paul had discipled Timothy, his son in the things of the Lord, he urged Timothy to teach the great truths of God's Word to trustworthy men who would, in turn, pass them on to others (2 Tim. 2:2).

COUNSEL

The goal of discipling is, of course, to make disciples. But before beginning this important task, we need to know what a disciple is.

Characteristics of a disciple

FAITH:
A disciple is one who has put his faith in Jesus Christ for eternal salvation and continues to live by faith (John 3:16; Rom. 1:17; Heb. 11:6).

Disciples are known as "believers" because of their faith in Christ (Acts 2:44).

Disciples grow in their faith because they read the Bible (John 20:31; Rom. 10:17; 2 Pet. 3:18).

OBEDIENCE:
Disciples live as Jesus has taught them to, and find that obedience is not a form of bondage but the beginning of true freedom (John 8:30, 31).

Obedience is proof that a disciple has faith, a faith that is not "dead and useless" (James 2:17).

Obedience is a demonstration of his love for Christ (John 14:24).

HOPE:
The disciple has a hope that looks forward to the salvation God has promised, and knows that it is his without question (Heb. 11:23).

The disciple knows that Christ is his only hope. The hope of glory (1 Tim. 1:1; Col. 1:27).

The disciple has the Holy Spirit's power within him, causing him to overflow with hope (Rom. 15:13).

The disciple looks forward to the time when he will see the glory of Christ, and this belief in Christ's return is why he tries to stay pure (Titus 2:13; 1 John 3:3).

THE DISCIPLE HAS:
A hope that endures in times of trouble (Rom. 12:12); a hope of becoming all that God has in mind for him to be (Rom. 5:2); a hope of a better life after this one (1 Cor. 15:19); a hope of a new body that will never become sick or die (Rom. 8:23, 24); a hope of a better world (Rom. 8:18-21); a hope of a home with Jesus in heaven.

Obstacles to becoming a disciple

PRIDE OF PERSONAL PIETY:
I can do it myself (Luke 18:1-14, 17).

LOVE OF EARTHLY POSSESSIONS:
I have too much to lose (Luke 18:18-27).

FEAR OF PERSONAL INJURY:
I don't want to take any chances (Luke 18:31-34; Matt. 16:21-25).

PRAYER
Pray that the believer will truly become a disciplined follower of Jesus Christ and will teach others to follow him.

FOLLOW-UP
Carefully study the Scriptures referred to in this chapter. Determine that you will be a life-long disciple of Jesus Christ. Begin thinking of others that you can encourage to become true disciples.

————————————
————————————
————————————
————————————
————————————
————————————
————————————
————————————
————————————
————————————
————————————
————————————
————————————
————————————
————————————
————————————
————————————
————————————
————————————
————————————

SCRIPTURE

Matthew 28:19, 20
Therefore go and make disci-ples in all the nations, baptiz-ing them into the name of the Father and of the Son and of the Holy Spirit, and then teach these new disciples to obey all the commands I have given you; and be sure of this—that I am with you always, even to the end of the world.

Acts 1:8
But when the Holy Spirit has come upon you, you will re-ceive power to testify about me with great effect, to the people in Jerusalem, throughout Judea, in Samaria, and to the ends of the earth, about my death and resurrection.

John 14:12, 13
In solemn truth I tell you, anyone believing in me shall do the same miracles I have done, and even greater ones, because I am going to be with the Father. You can ask him for anything, *using my name, and I will do it, for this will bring praise to the Father because of what I, the Son, will do for you.*

John 16:14
He shall praise me and bring me great honor by showing you my glory.

DESCRIPTION

Witnessing is the act of telling others about what you have experienced. In the context of Christian-ity, it involves testifying to others of the forgive-ness, love, deliverance, power, and peace of knowing Jesus Christ as Savior.

BIBLICAL PERSPECTIVE

Jesus' last instructions to his disciples before he ascended to his Father were in relation to wit-nessing. He commissioned them to go into all the world and make disciples. He promised them that when they received the Holy Spirit from the Father, they would become witnesses of all that they had seen and heard. And today, as we witness, the Lord confirms his Word with signs and authority (Mark 16:20; Matt. 28:19, 20).

COUNSEL

When a person has experienced the forgiveness of his sins, he is then able to witness or give testimony to his salvation, found in Jesus Christ. This does not necessarily make one an evangelist (Eph. 4:11), but makes one equivalent to the witnesses in the early church. They said, "We cannot stop telling about the wonderful things we saw Jesus do and heard him say" (Acts 4:20). We share this authority as we too know him person-ally.

The power to witness is given as a result of the work of the Holy Spirit (Mark 16:17-20). The willingness to witness is a decision each one must make.

Tell the counselee: The message to share is the best witness you can share. It is not just teaching Bible truths. It is being a *product* of those truths. In other words, don't just say the gospel message—be it and do it.

PRAYER

Pray that God will anoint the counselee with the Holy Spirit, equipping him for witnessing. You may have to pray that he be released from the bondage of fear or feelings of not being good enough to share Jesus with others. The general direction of your prayer for him should be to encourage him to share his faith freely and boldly.

REFERENCES

Psalm 14:3; Ecclesiastes 7:29
The guilt of man

Romans 5:10; Colossians 1:21; James 4:4
Separation from God

2 Thessalonians 1:8, 9; 2 Peter 3:7
God's judgment upon the ungodly

1 Timothy 2:5, 6; Hebrews 12:24
God's provision for man

John 14:6; Acts 4:12
Jesus is the way

Acts 5:31; 13:38, 26:18
Opportunity for repentance

Ephesians 4:32; 1 John 2:12
Forgiveness

Isaiah 1:18; 1 John 1:7; Revelation 7:14
Cleansing

Acts 13:39; Romans 3:24; 8:30
Justification

Titus 3:4-7
The work of Christ

Ephesians 2:8, 9; Titus 2:11; 3:4-7
By grace

1 Corinthians 13
Witness in love

READING
Christian Worker's New Testament

EMOTIONAL PROBLEMS

SCRIPTURE

Ephesians 4:31
Stop being mean, bad-tempered, and angry. Quarreling, harsh words, and dislike of others should have no place in your lives.

Colossians 3:8
But now is the time to cast off and throw away all these rotten garments of anger, hatred, cursing, and dirty language.

Proverbs 29:22
A hot-tempered man starts fights and gets into all kinds of trouble.

Ecclesiastes 7:9
Don't be quick-tempered— that is being a fool.

Matthew 5:22
But I have added to that rule, and tell you that if you are only angry, even in your own home, you are in danger of judgment! If you call your friend an idiot, you are in danger of being brought before the court. And if you curse him, you are in danger of the fires of hell.

Proverbs 19:11
A wise man restrains his anger and overlooks insults. This is to his credit.

_____

_____

_____

_____

PROBLEM

Anger is manifested when we yield to extreme pressures from people or circumstances and say or do something that offends others. This happens whenever we allow our flesh to control us rather than the Holy Spirit.

BIBLICAL PERSPECTIVE

The Bible admonishes us to stop our anger! Turn off our wrath. Don't fret and worry—it only leads to harm (Ps. 37:8). When we allow anger to control our lives we not only hurt others, but we hurt ourselves by destroying our witness before God and man.

COUNSEL

When anger is manifested in a person's life, totally yielding to the Holy Spirit will replace that anger with God's love and bring about reconciliation.

It makes no difference what someone has said or done or the circumstances that are encountered. According to God's Word we are to "listen, all of you. Love your enemies. Do good to those who hate you. Pray for the happiness of those who curse you; implore God's blessing on those who hurt you" (Luke 6:27, 28).

Jesus set the supreme example as he hung dying on the cross at Calvary. By the world's standards, he had every right to be angry toward those who placed him there, yet he asked the Father to forgive them.

If Jesus, at the point of death, was able to forgive, then there is no freedom for us to exhibit anger toward people or circumstances that seem unfair.

We are reminded in God's Word how important forgiveness is in our lives. In Matthew 6:14, 15 we are told that "Your heavenly Father will forgive you if you forgive those who sin against you; but if you refuse to forgive them, he will not forgive you."

By our godly response to those who would cause anger to rise up within us, we can be a part of the Holy Spirit's work in convicting them and completing God's work in them.

The following guidelines will assist someone in overcoming anger.

1. Recognize unchecked anger as sin. "Be kind to each other, tenderhearted, forgiving one another, just as God has forgiven you" (Eph. 4:32).
2. Confess it as sin. "But if we confess our sins to him, he can be depended on to forgive us and to cleanse us from every wrong" (1 John 1:9).
3. Receive God's grace and release. "And if we really know he is listening when we talk to him and make our requests, then we can be sure that he will answer us" (1 John 5:15).
4. Ask God to fill you with his Holy Spirit. "And if even sinful persons like yourselves give children what they need, don't you realize that your heavenly Father will do at least as much, and give the Holy Spirit to those who ask for him?" (Luke 11:13).

PRAYER

Encourage counselees to ask for God's forgiveness and help in loving and forgiving those that have offended them. They need to thank and praise God for the victory over anger and for the healing of relationships.

READING

Spirit-Controlled Temperament by Tim LaHaye

Ephesians 4:26, 27
If you are angry, don't sin by nursing your grudge. Don't let the sun go down with you still angry—get over it quickly; for when you are angry you give a mighty foothold to the devil.

REFERENCES

Proverbs 14:17
A short-tempered man is a fool. He hates the man who is patient.

Proverbs 14:29
A wise man controls his temper. He knows that anger causes mistakes.

Proverbs 15:18
A quick-tempered man starts fights; a cool-tempered man tries to stop them.

Colossians 3:21
Fathers, don't scold your children so much that they become discouraged and quit trying.

_____

_____

_____

_____

_____

_____

_____

_____

SCRIPTURE

Romans 8:31, 32
What can we ever say to such wonderful things as these? If God is on our side, who can ever be against us? Since he did not spare even his own Son for us but gave him up for us all, won't he also surely give us everything else?

Philippians 4:6-9
Don't worry about anything; instead, pray about everything; tell God your needs and don't forget to thank him for his answers. If you do this you will experience God's peace, which is far more wonderful than the human mind can understand. His peace will keep your thoughts and your hearts quiet and at rest as you trust in Christ Jesus. And now, brothers, as I close this letter let me say this one more thing: Fix your thoughts on what is true and good and right. Think about things that are pure and lovely, and dwell on the fine, good things in others. Think about all you can praise God for and be glad about. Keep putting into practice all you learned from me and saw me doing, and the God of peace will be with you.

PROBLEM

Mental distress or agitation results from legitimate concern over a real or imagined problem that has grown out of proportion. Worry grips us when we allow our old sinful nature, which is the enemy of God, to convince us that God isn't quite big enough to get us through this problem.

BIBLICAL PERSPECTIVE

Jesus told his disciples not to worry about even their basic needs, because God, the heavenly Father, knows our needs and delights in providing for us. He simply wants us to give him first place in our lives (Matt. 6:31-33). We must let God have all our worries and cares; he is watching everything that concerns us (1 Pet. 5:7).

COUNSEL

Worry is a sin which must be confessed. The place to begin is 1 John 1:9. God demands that we agree with him when he tells us our worry is uncalled for and is a sin against him. To deny that our worry is sin is to fool ourselves and call God a liar. If we confess our sins, God will forgive and cleanse us from the wrong in our lives (1 John 1:8-10).

Worry is limited faith that must be increased. When you worry, you insult God, because it is your way of saying, "God, you're just not big enough to handle this problem in my life." Several times Jesus said, "O men of little faith!" He must have been insulted and angry because those men who knew him best continued to worry about problems which were so easy for him to solve. Don't continue in this sin of faithlessness. Replace your worry with a growing faith. Here's how: "Faith comes from listening to this Good News— the Good News about Christ." When you read the stories of what Jesus has done for so many needy people you'll find that to trust him for the problems you're facing is a lot easier.

Worry is a habit which must be changed. Like any other bad habit, it must be replaced by a good habit. Remember, the definition of worry is: "Mental distress or agitation. . . ." So, in order to be freed of this habitual mental distress, you must learn, with God's help, to habitually think on good things. Guidelines for thinking are found in Philippians 4:8.

PRAYER

Encourage those who worry to thank God and acknowledge that he will never leave or forsake them and is always watching everything that concerns them. Have them make a commitment to God to read his Word and pray daily and fix their thoughts on what is true and good and right.

REFERENCES

Joshua 1:9
Worrying doesn't do any good, but trusting God does

Psalm 34:4
The Lord can free you from all your fears

Psalm 127:1, 2
Why worry? God will help you

Proverbs 12:25
Anxious hearts are heavy and need encouragement

Luke 12:22-34
Worrying doesn't do any good, but trusting God does

1 Corinthians 10:13
When you are tempted to worry, God will help you stand against it

James 1:2-5
Your problems aren't the end of the world, but the beginning of God's blessing

1 Peter 5:7
Let him have all your worries and cares, for he is always thinking about you and watching everything that concerns you.

Hebrews 13:5, 6
Stay away from the love of money; be satisfied with what you have. For God has said, "I will never, never fail you nor forsake you." That is why we can say without any doubt or fear, "The Lord is my Helper and I am not afraid of anything that mere man can do to me."

SCRIPTURE

Matthew 6:14, 15
Your heavenly Father will forgive you if you forgive those who sin against you; but if you refuse to forgive them, he will not forgive you.

Romans 12:14-21
If someone mistreats you because you are a Christian, don't curse him; pray that God will bless him. When others are happy, be happy with them. If they are sad, share their sorrow. Work happily together. Don't try to act big. Don't try to get into the good graces of important people, but enjoy the company of ordinary folks. And don't think you know it all!

Never pay back evil for evil. Do things in such a way that everyone can see you are honest clear through. Don't quarrel with anyone. Be at peace with everyone, just as much as possible.

Dear friends, never avenge yourselves. Leave that to God, for he has said that he will repay those who deserve it. [Don't take the law into your own hands.] Instead, feed your enemy if he is hungry. If he is thirsty give him something to drink and you will be "heaping coals of fire on his head." In other words, he will feel ashamed of himself for what he has done to you. Don't let evil get the upper hand but conquer evil by doing good.

PROBLEM

Everyone of us, at some time or another, feels that he has been wronged by another person. At that point he will either forgive or become bitter and resentful. Bitterness will steal his inner peace and can even cause physical illness. It will destroy his fellowship with God and cause his closest human relationships to suffer.

BIBLICAL PERSPECTIVE

Bitterness and resentment are sins which have no place in the believer's life. Jesus plainly states that those who refuse to forgive others will not be forgiven (Matt. 6:14, 15). Paul tells us that if you love someone, you won't hold a grudge against him (1 Cor. 13:5).

COUNSEL

If the one who is bitter and resentful has never trusted Christ as Savior, that is where to begin. Those who know they are forgiven are then able to forgive others. Explain how to receive Christ as Savior and Lord, and invite this person to confess his sins to God and trust Christ now.

If he is a Christian, urge him to confess his sin of bitterness and be cleansed by the blood of Christ (1 John 1:9). He needs to recognize how serious a matter it is to hold a grudge against the one who has wronged him (Matt. 6:14, 15).

Point out that he needs to replace that bitterness with love, for "love does not hold grudges and will hardly even notice when others do it wrong" (1 Cor. 13:5). And that love itself is something he can demonstrate only as the Holy Spirit produces it in his heart and life. "But when the Holy Spirit controls our lives he will produce this kind of fruit in us: love, joy, peace, patience, kindness, goodness . . ." (Gal. 5:22).

Encourage him to follow God's example by showing love, in some practical way, for that person who has wronged him. "But God showed his great love for us by sending Christ to die for us while we were still sinners" (Rom. 5:8).

PRAYER
Have counselees thank the Lord for not holding grudges against them, but forgiving and forgetting every time they confess their sins to him. Encourage them to ask the Lord to help them be like him, able to forgive others, no matter what they have done.

REFERENCES

Anger
Matthew 5:22
Ephesians 4:26
Ephesians 4:31
Colossians 3:8

Bitterness
Hebrews 12:15
James 3:14
Proverbs 23:17, 18
1 Corinthians 13:4
Galatians 5:24-26

Envy
Psalm 37:1
Proverbs 3:31
Matthew 27:18

Evil Planning
Isaiah 59:4-7
Matthew 27:23
John 12:10

Hatred
Leviticus 19:17
Proverbs 10:12
1 Corinthians 5:8
1 Peter 2:1
1 John 2:9
1 John 4:20

1 Corinthians 13:5
Love does not demand its own way. It is not irritable or touchy. It does not hold grudges and will hardly even notice when others do it wrong.

Ephesians 4:31, 32
Stop being mean, bad-tempered and angry. Quarreling, harsh words, and dislike of others should have no place in your lives. Instead, be kind to each other, tenderhearted, forgiving one another, just as God has forgiven you because you belong to Christ.

Hebrews 12:14, 15
Try to stay out of all quarrels and seek to live a clean and holy life, for one who is not holy will not see the Lord. Look after each other so that not one of you will fail to find God's best blessings. Watch out that no bitterness takes root among you, for as it springs up it causes deep trouble, hurting many in their spiritual lives.

1 Peter 2:19-23
Praise the Lord if you are punished for doing right! Of course, you get no credit for being patient if you are beaten for doing wrong; but if you do right and suffer for it, and are patient beneath the blows, God is well pleased.

SCRIPTURE

1 Corinthians 9:24-27
In a race, everyone runs but only one person gets first prize. So run your race to win. To win the contest you must deny yourselves many things that would keep you from doing your best. An athlete goes to all this trouble just to win a blue ribbon or a silver cup, but we do it for a heavenly reward that never disappears. So I run straight to the goal with purpose in every step. I fight to win. I'm not just shadow-boxing or playing around. Like an athlete I punish my body, treating it roughly, training it to do what it should, not what it wants to. Otherwise I fear that after enlisting others for the race, I myself might be declared unfit and ordered to stand aside.

1 Corinthians 10:13
But remember this—the wrong desires that come into your life aren't anything new and different. Many others have faced exactly the same problems before you. And no temptation is irresistible. You can trust God to keep the temptation from becoming so strong that you can't stand up against it, for he has promised this and will do what he says. He will show you how to escape temptation's power so that you can bear up patiently against it.

PROBLEM

Compulsiveness is defined as "an irresistible, repeated impulse to perform some irrational act." A few common examples of compulsive behavior are: gambling, sex, eating, talking, drinking alcoholic beverages or taking drugs, working, spending money, punishing children, etc. Some of the activities named are perfectly innocent in themselves and others are nearly always harmful. Whether an act is intrinsically right or wrong, it becomes wrong, and even dangerous, when performed compulsively. For instance, while there is nothing wrong with eating, the compulsive eater will become over-weight and suffer ill health.

BIBLICAL PERSPECTIVE

The Apostle Paul warns those who are compulsive: "But when you follow your own wrong inclinations your lives will produce these evil results. . . ." The list includes eagerness for lustful pleasure, murder, drunkenness, etc. (Gal. 5:19-21). But when the Holy Spirit is in control, he produces such fruit as love, peace, patience, goodness, and self-control (Gal. 5:22, 23).

COUNSEL

God understands us and knows how very much we need his help. Take a moment to reflect on Jeremiah 13:23: "Can the Ethiopian change the color of his skin? or a leopard take away his spots? Nor can you who are so used to doing evil now start being good." In order to change, the compulsive person needs to first make Jesus Christ his Savior and Lord. The one who has tried on his own to overcome compulsiveness will not find it hard to believe Jesus' claim that "apart from me you can't do a thing" (John 15:5). Prayerfully explain to this person how he can trust in Christ and become a child of God. But don't be surprised to find a Christian who still has a problem with compulsiveness. In Romans 7:22-25 the Apostle Paul describes his struggle and how he was set free by Christ: "I love to do God's will so far as my new nature is concerned; but there is something else deep within me, in my lower nature, that is at war with my mind and wins the fight and makes me a slave to the sin that is still within me. In my mind I want to be God's willing servant but instead I find myself still enslaved to sin. So you see how it is: my new life tells me to do right, but the old nature that is still inside me loves to sin. Oh, what a terrible predicament I'm in! Who will free me from my slavery to this deadly lower nature? Thank God! It has been done by Jesus Christ our Lord. He has set me free."

The Christian can overcome compulsive behavior as he follows these four scriptural principles:

Recognize that your old sin nature is dead. "So look upon your old sin nature as dead and unresponsive to sin, and instead be alive to God, alert to him, through Jesus Christ our Lord" (Rom. 6:11).

Thank the Lord for what he has done. "Thank God! It has been done by Jesus Christ our Lord. He has set me free" (Rom. 7:25).

Allow the Holy Spirit to control your life. "But when the Holy Spirit controls our lives he will produce this kind of fruit in us: love, joy, peace, patience, kindness, goodness, faithfulness, gentleness and self-control . . ." (Gal. 5:22, 23).

Cooperate with what Christ has accomplished in your life. "Do not let sin control your puny body any longer; do not give in to its sinful desires. Do

Galatians 5:16
I advise you to obey only the Holy Spirit's instructions. He will tell you where to go and what to do, and then you won't always be doing the wrong things your evil nature wants you to.

Galatians 5:19-23
But when you follow your own wrong inclinations your lives will produce these evil results . . . eagerness for lustful pleasure . . . hatred and fighting . . . jealousy . . . anger . . . constant effort to get the best for yourself . . . envy, murder, drunkenness, wild parties, and all that sort of thing. Let me tell you again as I have before, that anyone living that sort of life will not inherit the Kingdom of God.

But when the Holy Spirit controls our lives he will produce this kind of fruit in us: love, joy, peace, patience, kindness, goodness, faithfulness, gentleness and self-control. . . .

2 Peter 1:6
Next, learn to put aside your own desires so that you will become patient and godly, gladly letting God have his way with you.

FOLLOW-UP
Study the Scriptures quoted in this chapter. Memorize 1 Corinthians 10:13.

not let any part of your bodies become tools of wickedness, to be used for sinning; but give yourselves completely to God . . . to be used for his good purposes" (Rom. 6:12, 13).

"So I run straight to the goal with purpose in every step. I fight to win. I'm not just shadow-boxing or playing around. Like an athlete I punish my body, treating it roughly, training it to do what it should, not what it wants to. Otherwise I fear that after enlisting others for the race, I myself might be declared unfit and ordered to stand aside" (1 Cor. 9:26, 27).

Cooperation with Christ will include some tough decisions, like turning down an invitation to the dog track if you are a compulsive gambler, or to a cocktail party if you are an alcoholic. If you have a problem with pornography, you will have to stay away from certain areas of town where you might be tempted by the pornographic bookstores and theatres, and even the drug store's magazine rack may have to be avoided.

If you are a compulsive spender, you may find it helpful to destroy your charge cards. The compulsive eater may become stronger by joining a dieter's club where he is accountable to someone.

Jesus said, "So if your eye—even if it is your best eye!—causes you to lust, gouge it out and throw it away. . . . And if your hand—even your right hand—causes you to sin, cut it off and throw it away. . ." (Matt. 5:29, 30). What Jesus is saying, in the strongest language, is that you should do whatever is necessary to avoid compulsive behavior.

PRAYER
Pray that this one who is struggling with compulsive behavior will experience a new self-control in times of strong temptation.

PROBLEM

Depression is a prolonged feeling of sadness, discouragement, and an inability to "get on top of things." It is probably the most common emotional problem a counselor will encounter. The following symptoms may be present when a person is depressed:

PHYSICAL:
Insomnia, loss of appetite, loss of weight, loss of interest in sex, complaints about the body, lack of energy.

THINKING PATTERNS:
Difficulty concentrating, poor memory, trouble making decisions, excessive self-criticism, thoughts of death or suicide.

EMOTIONS:
Despair, guilt, irritability, crying, fear, gloomy outlook (sometimes masked by such opposite behavior as giddiness, inappropriate laughter, or pronounced quietness and sweetness).

ACTIVITY:
Slowing of most activity, withdrawal from social contacts, deterioration of work and personal appearance. Risk of suicide is strong for extremely depressed persons, as is the risk of mental or emotional breakdown.

BIBLICAL PERSPECTIVE

Discouragement can be caused by circumstances beyond a person's control: dead-end job, marital difficulties, criticism from friends and family, etc. It can also arise from a sense of failure or inadequacy, which could be caused even by seemingly insignificant factors in a person's life. These factors can gradually multiply into a grave problem with self-esteem.

Sometimes depression is rooted in sin, as seen in Psalm 38:3-8. With a prolonged feeling of sadness can come a growing distrust of God, resentment of others, and self-pity. These in turn can lead to guilt, inactivity, doubting, complaining, and worrying, so that the person may feel as though he's in an

SCRIPTURE

Psalm 51:10-12
Create in me a new, clean heart, O God, filled with clean thoughts and right desires. Don't toss me aside, banished forever from your presence. Don't take your Holy Spirit from me. Restore to me again the joy of your salvation, and make me willing to obey you.

Romans 8:28, 31
And we know that all that happens to us is working for our good if we love God and are fitting into his plans. What can we ever say to such wonderful things as these? If God is on our side, who can ever be against us?

1 Thessalonians 5:18
No matter what happens, always be thankful, for this is God's will for you who belong to Christ Jesus.

Matthew 11:28-30
Come to me and I will give you rest—all of you who work so hard beneath a heavy yoke. Wear my yoke—for it fits perfectly—and let me teach you; for I am gentle and humble, and you shall find rest for your souls; for I give you only light burdens.

Isaiah 50:7
Because the Lord God helps me, I will not be dismayed; therefore, I have set my face like flint to do his will, and I know that I will triumph.

inescapable pit. Many admirable biblical characters experienced discouragement, but the Bible gives evidence that hope in God's mercy and steadfast love provides deliverance from depression.

COUNSEL

Recognize and take seriously the depth of the depression. Don't give such glib responses as "Cheer up," "Snap out of it," "It can't be that bad," or "You shouldn't feel this way." Better responses are: "I can tell this is really bothering you," "Tell me about it," or "I want to help you."

Try to find out how the depression began and how long it has lasted. If the person is inarticulate about the problem areas in his life, ask about these areas:

- Relationships with spouse, children, parents, church relatives, neighbors, coworkers;
- Physical problems such as insomnia, aging, problems with drugs or alcohol, obesity, and (for women) menstruation and menopause;
- Disorganization in the home or on the job, resulting in conflicts with family members or fellow workers;
- Self-condemnation arising from guilt over dishonesty, sexual sins, failure to witness, or failure to fulfill responsibilities;
- Financial problems resulting from gambling, bad investments, family emergencies, and so on;
- Loneliness.

The depressed person needs to be assured that God cares. This is the best a counselor can do, since it is probably beyond our power to remedy the person's physical or financial problems, though we can refer the person to others who are knowledgeable in these areas. Depression caused by agonizing over sins can be dealt with by confession and repentance. (See the sections in this handbook on REPENTANCE and on the various moral problems over which a person may experience guilt.) Whatever the cause of the depression, refer the person to biblical confessions of faith in God's ability to overcome human difficulties. These include Philippians 4:13, Philemon 4:19, 2 Timothy 1:7, Romans 12:3, Romans 8:37, Luke 10:19, and 1 Peter 2:24.

If possible, arrange for a referral to a competent pastor or Christian counselor. Encourage the person to pray, study the Bible, and fellowship with other Christians in a Christ-centered church that clearly teaches the Bible.

PRAYER
Prayer for the counselee should include confession of sins, forgiveness of others, thanks for God's love, and request for healing and renewed joy in life.

REFERENCES

Psalm 42:4-11
God's love for us

Philippians 4:4-13
Rejoicing in the Lord

Hebrews 4:14-16
God is touched by our feelings

James 4:8
Repentance assures God's presence

READING
Prison to Praise by Merlin Carothers
How to Win over Depression by Tim LaHaye
How to Help a Friend by Paul Welter
Understanding a Woman's Depression by Brenda Poinsett

SCRIPTURE

Joshua 1:5-9
No one will be able to oppose you as long as you live, for I will be with you just as I was with Moses; I will not abandon you or fail to help you.

Be strong and brave, for you will be a successful leader of my people; and they shall conquer all the land I promised to their ancestors. You need only to be strong and courageous and to obey to the letter every law Moses gave you, for if you are careful to obey every one of them you will be successful in everything you do. Constantly remind the people about these laws, and you yourself must think about them every day and every night so that you will be sure to obey all of them. For only then will you succeed. Yes, be bold and strong! Banish fear and doubt! For remember, the Lord your God is with you wherever you go.

Psalm 23:4
Even when walking through the dark valley of death I will not be afraid, for you are close beside me, guarding, guiding all the way.

Isaiah 41:10
Fear not, for I am with you. Do not be dismayed. I am your God. I will strengthen you; I will help you; I will uphold you with my victorious right hand.

PROBLEM

Fear is a universal problem. From infancy to the grave we experience all kinds of fears and insecurities. Though most of our fears are unfounded, they gnaw at us day and night. They weaken our hearts, rob our peace of mind, sap our energy, hinder our work, and gradually erode our relationships. Only Jesus Christ can set us free from the bondage of fear.

BIBLICAL PERSPECTIVE

God, the Commander of the heavenly armies, is here among us. Jesus, who has all authority in heaven and earth, has promised to be with us always, even to the end of the world. So we need not fear no matter what happens (Ps. 46; Matt. 28:18-20).

COUNSEL

The counsel in this chapter is primarily for the Christian. The one who has not trusted Christ as Lord and Savior has good reason for fear (Rev. 20:10-15); urge him to open the door of his heart and let Jesus come in (Rev. 3:20).

The Christian has no reason to live in fear. There are steps he can take to overcome fear and enjoy real freedom in Christ.

Three steps toward overcoming fear:

Identify the fear. We cannot expect to win the battle until we have first identified the enemy. Too often we allow vague, undefined fears to immobilize us. What is it you fear?

Consider the worst thing that could happen. Is it really that bad, or has the mind created a frightening but impotent monster? Sometimes, when we think through the ramifications of our situation, we wonder why we were ever so terrified. That thing I fear—is it a monster or a mouse?

Claim the truths of God's Word. Jesus said, "The truth will set you free" (John 8:32). So, claim the truth that best fits your situation.

When you fear:	Claim:
New responsibilities and challenges	Joshua 1:5-9
Enemies and dangerous situations	Psalms 23:4; 27:1-3
Natural disasters and war	Psalm 46
Spiritual battles	Ephesians 6:10-18
Interpersonal relationships	2 Timothy 1:6, 7
Death	1 Corinthians 15:54-57; 2 Corinthians 5:8
The unknown	Psalm 23

PRAYER

Pray that Jesus Christ will set the counselee free from all of his fears and that he will be used of God to give courage to others.

_____
_____
_____
_____
_____
_____
_____
_____
_____
_____
_____
_____
_____

Psalm 27:1-3
The Lord is my light and my salvation; he protects me from danger—whom shall I fear? When evil men come to destroy me, they will stumble and fall! Yes, though a mighty army marches against me, my heart shall know no fear! I am confident that God will save me.

Psalm 34:1-4
I will praise the Lord no matter what happens. I will constantly speak of his glories and grace. . . . Let all who are discouraged take heart. . . .
For I cried to him and he answered me! He freed me from all my fears.

Psalm 46:1, 2
God is our refuge and strength, a tested help in times of trouble. And so we need not fear. . . .

John 16:33
I have told you all this so that you will have peace of heart and mind.

Romans 8:31
What can we ever say to such wonderful things as these? If God is on our side, who can ever be against us?

2 Timothy 1:7
For the Holy Spirit, God's gift, does not want you to be afraid of people, but to be wise and strong, and to love them and enjoy being with them.

SCRIPTURE

Psalm 103:10-12
He has not punished us as we deserve for all our sins, for his mercy toward those who fear and honor him is as great as the height of the heavens above the earth. He has removed our sins as far away from us as the east is from the west.

Isaiah 43:25
I, yes, I alone am he who blots away your sins for my own sake and will never think of them again.

Matthew 6:14
Your heavenly Father will forgive you if you forgive those who sin against you.

John 20:22, 23
Then he breathed on them and told them, "Receive the Holy Spirit. If you forgive anyone's sins, they are forgiven. If you refuse to forgive them, they are unforgiven."

_____

_____

_____

_____

_____

_____

_____

PROBLEM

This problem may include a need for (1) God's forgiveness of sin and repentance leading to salvation, or renewal in a Christian; (2) the forgiveness of others in order to be in God's will—essential for spiritual, mental, and physical health and well-being.

BIBLICAL PERSPECTIVE

To love the Lord with one's heart, mind, soul, and strength, and one's neighbor as oneself, is to have experienced forgiveness and to have forgiven others as well. (See the Lord's Prayer, Matthew 6:12.)

COUNSEL

As you seek the Lord for wisdom, pray for words to say which will encourage a heart of forgiveness. If the person is already a Christian, be open to the Spirit revealing unconfessed sin to him. Take seriously the person's feelings of guilt, and guide him toward true repentance.

If the problem is forgiveness of others, the person needs to truly forgive and ask God to forgive both himself and that other person. When forgiven, the other person is released from the bondage of this person's condemnation. What we bind is truly bound, and what we loose is loosed (John 20:22, 23). Once this is accomplished, the burden of guilt is replaced by freedom and joy.

After knowing God has forgiven, and after forgiving others from whom we have experienced wrong, then we can rejoice that God is doing a new thing (Isa. 43:18, 19), and offer him sacrifices of praise (Heb. 13:15).

PRAYER
Pray for God's forgiving Spirit to anoint the counselee, and rejoice in praises to God in the person's behalf.

READING
The Freedom of Forgiveness by David Augsburger
Forgive and Forget: Healing the Hurts We Don't Deserve by Lewis B. Smedes

_____

_____

_____

_____

_____

_____

REFERENCES
Forgive and be forgiven
Matthew 6:14
Mark 11:25
Ephesians 4:32
Isaiah 43:25
John 20:22, 23
Colossians 3:13
Galatians 6:1, 2
Isaiah 43:18, 19
Philippians 3:13
1 John 1:9
Jeremiah 18:4
Matthew 18:21, 22

Also see:
Hebrews 8:12
1 John 2:1, 2

SCRIPTURE

John 14:1-3
Let not your heart be troubled. You are trusting God, now trust in me. There are many homes up there where my Father lives, and I am going to prepare them for your coming. When everything is ready, then I will come and get you, so that you can always be with me where I am. If this weren't so, I would tell you plainly.

1 Corinthians 13:12
In the same way, we can see and understand only a little about God now, as if we were peering at his reflection in a poor mirror; but someday we are going to see him in his completeness, face to face. Now all that I know is hazy and blurred, but then I will see everything clearly, just as clearly as God sees into my heart right now.

John 11:25
Jesus told her, "I am the one who raises the dead and gives them life again. Anyone who believes in me, even though he dies like anyone else, shall live again."

Philippians 1:25
Yes, I am still needed down here and so I feel certain I will be staying on earth a little longer, to help you grow and become happy in your faith.

PROBLEM

Grief is the depressing sorrow or pain caused by the loss of a loved one.

BIBLICAL PERSPECTIVE

It is the lot of man that he should grieve over the loss of loved ones. For the Christian, the hope we have in Jesus Christ carries us through any times of sorrow or pain (1 Thess. 4:13). Times of mourning can be times when the lost can see the need to be saved and Christians can be reminded of the brevity of life and the hope of eternal life.

COUNSEL

If the counselee is grieving over a departed Christian, refer to the Scriptures above. Comfort and assurance of God's love and concern are needed. Be sensitive to the counselee's feelings and remind him that, though grief is natural and appropriate, we can find joy and hope in believing that the loved one is with Christ.

If the counselee is not a Christian, take this opportunity to lead the person to salvation. Speak of the need for those of us who are now alive to prepare to meet God. Encourage the counselee to worship in a Christ-centered church that clearly teaches the Bible and start growing in understanding, wisdom, and knowledge.

Very deep grief is often experienced because of the death of a child. Even mature Christians have difficulty understanding why a loving God would allow an innocent child to die. The counselor is not obliged to explain God's action, since we do not fully understand the purpose in such cases. However, it may be appropriate to refer to 1 Kings 14:1-13, the story of Abijah, the son of Jeroboam. God said he was taking the child because he saw some good thing in him. Also, David's experience of losing a son is helpful to remember. David hoped in God and prayed that the child would not die (2 Sam. 12:13-23), but when the child died, David knew he had to go on with the business of living. This was not callousness but mature coping, accepting circumstances and going on to live a life in fellowship with God.

PRAYER

Pray for God's comfort for the counselee and his family. Ask God to allow his peace to fill their hearts during these dark hours.

REFERENCES

1 Corinthians 15
The resurrection of believers

Psalm 23
The Lord is our shepherd

2 Corinthians 5:1-9
Looking forward to heaven

1 Peter 1:3-6
Hope of eternal life

READING

A Grief Observed by C. S. Lewis
Beyond Heartache by Mari Hanes and Jack Hayford
For Those Who Grieve by R. Earl Allen
Life, Death, and Beyond by J. Kerby Anderson

Romans 8:35, 37
Who can ever keep Christ's love from us? When we have trouble or calamity, when we are hunted down or destroyed, is it because he doesn't love us anymore? And if we are hungry, or penniless, or in danger, or threatened with death, has God deserted us?

2 Corinthians 1:3, 4
What a wonderful God we have—he is the Father of our Lord Jesus Christ, the source of every mercy, and the one who so wonderfully comforts and strengthens us in our hardships and trials. And why does he do this? So that when others are troubled, needing our sympathy and encouragement, we can pass on to them this same help and comfort God has given us.

SCRIPTURE

Romans 3:19, 23
So, the judgment of God lies very heavily upon the Jews, for they are responsible to keep God's laws instead of doing all these evil things; not one of them has any excuse; in fact, all the world stands hushed and guilty before Almighty God.

Yes, all have sinned; all fall short of God's glorious ideal.

Romans 6:23
For the wages of sin is death, but the free gift of God is eternal life through Jesus Christ our Lord.

Ephesians 1:4
Long ago, even before he made the world, God chose us to be his very own, through what Christ would do for us; he decided then to make us holy in his eyes, without a single fault—we who stand before him covered with his love.

1 Peter 1:16
So be truly glad! There is wonderful joy ahead, even though the going is rough for a while down here.

Isaiah 44:22
I've blotted out your sins; they are gone like morning mist at noon! Oh, return to me, for I have paid the price to set you free.

PROBLEM

The counselee has said, thought, or done something that was wrong and against God's commandments. The Holy Spirit then convicts the counselee of the sin, and if he is obedient, the Spirit brings about repentance, change, and freedom from guilt.

BIBLICAL PERSPECTIVE

Every one of us stands guilty before God because we have broken his laws and fall short of his glorious ideal. Even those who seem relatively good in their behavior fall short and are seen by God as guilty of breaking His laws (Rom. 3:19, 23; James 2:10).

COUNSEL
How to deal with guilt:

Understand what it means to be guilty. The Bible clearly teaches that guilty sinners deserve to be punished, separated from God for all of eternity. God is holy and cannot allow sin in his presence (Rev. 20:12-15).

Marvel at how good God is to us. "But God showed his great love for us by sending Christ to die for us while we were still sinners" (Rom. 5:8).

"Without the shedding of blood there is no forgiveness of sins" (Heb. 9:22).

"He is the one who took God's wrath against our sins upon himself, and brought us into fellowship with God; and he is the forgiveness for our sins, and not only ours but all the world's" (1 John 2:2).

We must never take sin lightly—Christ died because of it.

Turn away from all sin. "From then on, Jesus began to preach. 'Turn from sin, and turn to God . . .' " (Matt. 4:17).

Jesus said, "Yet there is one thing wrong; you don't love me as at first! Think about those times of your first love (how different now!) and turn back to me again . . ." (Rev. 2:4, 5).

"But if we confess our sins to him, he can be depended on to forgive us and to cleanse us from every wrong. (And it is perfectly proper for God to do this for us because Christ died to wash away our sins)" (1 John 1:9).

If you are not a Christian, now is the time to turn from your sins and become a child of God. If you have already trusted in Christ for eternal salvation, but are guilty of sinning against him, turn away from your sins and be restored to that first love and fellowship you knew with Christ.

Thank God for his loving-kindness. "I will sing of the Lord's great love forever; with my mouth I will make your faithfulness known through all generations" (Ps. 89:1, NIV).

"Thank God for his Son—his Gift too wonderful for words" (2 Cor. 9:15).

God loves to hear his children say thank you.

Forget all your past sins. Paul wrote: "No, dear brothers, I am still not all I should be but I am bringing all my energies to bear on this one thing: Forgetting the past and looking forward to what lies ahead, I strain to reach the end of the race and receive the prize for which God is calling us up to heaven because of what Christ Jesus did for us" (Phil. 3:13, 14).

Our sins are dead and buried; so God doesn't want us to dig them up again.

Resist the guilt Satan tries to impose on you. "So give yourselves humbly to God. Resist the devil and he will flee from you" (James 4:7).

"Who will bring any charge against those whom God has chosen? It is God who justifies. Who is he that condemns? Christ Jesus, who

Romans 8:1-3
So there is now no condemnation awaiting those who belong to Christ Jesus. For the power of the life-giving Spirit—and this power is mine through Christ Jesus—has freed me from the vicious circle of sin and death. We aren't saved from sin's grasp by knowing the commandments of God, because we can't and don't keep them, but God put into effect a different plan to save us. He sent his own Son in a human body like ours—except that ours are sinful—and destroyed sin's control over us by giving himself as a sacrifice for our sins.

died—more than that, who was raised to life—is at the right hand of God and is also interceding for us" (Rom. 8:33, 34, NIV).

If you're letting Satan make you feel guilty, you need to stand on God's Word, which tells us there is no condemnation for those who are in Christ Jesus (Rom. 8:1). King David knew what it meant to be forgiven: "What joys when sins are covered over! What relief for those who have confessed their sins and God has cleared their record" (Ps. 32:1).

PRAYER
Encourage the counselee to thank the Lord for his wonderful plan to rid him of his guilt by placing it all on Jesus Christ, the Lamb of God. Have him confess all known sin. Pray that peace will flood his heart and that his cup will overflow with the joy of Christ. Pray for him to have opportunities, boldness, and wisdom to share the Good News of forgiveness with others who need to hear it.

FOLLOW-UP
Study all Scriptures referred to in this chapter. Remember, the truth will set you free (John 8:36).

PROBLEM

Inability to sleep accompanied by, or as a result of, burdens: sickness, financial worries, old age, grief, depression, or other causes.

BIBLICAL PERSPECTIVE

Salvation in Christ should enable us to lie down peacefully and sleep soundly, dwelling in safety (Ps. 4:8). God desires for his children to have safety and health in all their habits.

COUNSEL

Be aware that the underlying causes of insomnia are important in counseling and ministering to this person. As you talk and pray together with the counselee, the Spirit may impress upon you the root causes so that you can pray for specific healing of hurts that hinder true rest.

After initial sessions, you may find the person calling again and again, still unable to rest peacefully. Intercede for him, binding any power Satan may have over the situation, in the name and authority of Jesus. Pray for health and wholeness, offering praise that the answer will come. (See other sections of this handbook for ways to deal specifically with the underlying causes of sleeplessness: fear, anxiety, etc.)

PRAYER

Pray in Christ's authority and power. Praise and thank God for victory over sleeplessness.

SCRIPTURE

Psalm 3:5
Then I lay down and slept in peace and woke up safely, for the Lord was watching over me.

Psalm 4:8
I will lie down in peace and sleep, for though I am alone, O Lord, you will keep me safe.

Psalm 127:2
It is senseless for you to work so hard from early morning until late at night, fearing you will starve to death; for God wants his loved ones to get their proper rest.

Proverbs 3:24-26
With them on guard you can sleep without fear, you need not be afraid of disaster or the plots of wicked men, for the Lord is with you, he protects you.

Jeremiah 31:26
(Then Jeremiah wakened. "Such sleep is very sweet!" he said.)

Matthew 11:28
Come to me and I will give you rest—all of you who work so hard beneath a heavy yoke.

Isaiah 26:3
He will keep in perfect peace all those who trust in him, whose thoughts turn often to the Lord!

SCRIPTURE

Isaiah 54:10
*For the mountains may de-
part and the hills disappear,
but my kindness shall not
leave you. My promise of
peace for you will never be
broken, says the Lord who
has mercy upon you.*

Hebrews 13:5, 6
*Stay away from the love of
money; be satisfied with what
you have. For God has said,
"I will never, never fail you
nor forsake you." That is why
we can say without any doubt
or fear, "The Lord is my
Helper and I am not afraid of
anything that mere man can
do to me."*

1 Corinthians 1:9
*God will surely do this for
you, for he always does just
what he says, and he is the
one who invited you into this
wonderful friendship with his
Son, even Christ our Lord.*

Revelation 3:20
*Look! I have been standing
at the door and I am con-
stantly knocking. If anyone
hears me calling him and
opens the door, I will come in
and fellowship with him and
he with me.*

Psalm 34:18
*The Lord is close to those
whose hearts are breaking;
he rescues those who are humbly sorry for their sins.*

PROBLEM

Loneliness usually refers to the lack of com-
panionship and fellowship. Lonely persons feel
sad or dejected, and the sadness may be manifested in melancholy sighing, feeling worthless,
crying easily, self-pity, anxiety, and restlessness.

BIBLICAL PERSPECTIVE

God has promised never to leave nor forsake his
children (Heb. 13:5). We may often face times
when we stand alone among men, but we need
never stand without God. He is the Holy One
who is God of the universe, yet he is also the
constant companion and guide of each of us. The
Holy Spirit will comfort us and walk alongside us,
even in loneliness (John 16:7, 8).

COUNSEL

The well-worn cliché is true: If one acts as a
friend, one will have a friend. But the Christian
needs more than just a friend who can fill up gaps
of time and dispel loneliness. The Christian
needs Christian friends who can encourage
spiritual growth and effectual service in doing the
work of the kingdom. More than other people,
Christians can cure loneliness by showing that
service to others (and to God) brings us into
close contact with others and draws us out of our
self-pity. As long as we are wallowing in self-
absorption, we are unlikely to dispel our loneliness or be of much benefit to other human
beings. But Christians can encourage each other
in the life of self-emptying, which is the only
route to self-fulfillment.

Encourage the counselee to look for a Christ-
centered church that clearly teaches the Bible.
Point out the counselee's own worth and how he
is needed in the body of Christ. Point out also

that Jesus is a friend who will stick closer than a
brother, and who came that we might have life
full of meaning and purpose (John 10:10).

Remind the counselee that most churches and
church-related agencies need persons to do
volunteeer work in many capacities. Involvement
in such work leads to meeting new people and to
renewing one's zeal for Christian service.

Shut-ins almost always desire more companion-
ship. You might want to refer the counselee to a
church or group that provides food, flowers, or
just visits to shut-ins.

Involvement in a prayer group or prayer chain
is a way of drawing a person out of himself and
bringing him into meaningful contact with others.

If the counselee is not a Christian, try to lead
him to make a commitment to Christ. Assure
him that there are Christian fellowships where
warmth is extended to new people and where
there will be opportunities for making friends and
serving others. Refer him to a pastor or other
church leader at a church that is Christ-centered
and clearly teaches the Bible.

PRAYER
Pray that self-pity will be dispelled and that the
person will see the need not only for companion-
ship (which is a legitimate need) but for helping
others. Pray that the God who desires abundant
life for his people will fill the counselee with
perfect peace.

FOLLOW-UP
The counselee should make a list of people he
knows with needs of salvation, of deliverance
from particular sins, and so on. He should ask for
God's touch upon these persons.

Suggest that the counselee become a friend to

prisoners by writing them letters as a friend. He can encourage prisoners, pray for their concerns, and also request that they pray for his concerns. Praying for prisoners, for the church, for the oppressed—in short, praying for anyone—helps a person out of the rut of self-pity.

READING
Liberation from Loneliness by David Claerbaut

FAMILY

SCRIPTURE

Deuteronomy 6:5-7
You must love him with all your heart, soul, and might. And you must think constantly about these commandments I am giving you today. You must teach them to your children and talk about them when you are at home or out for a walk; at bedtime and the first thing in the morning.

Proverbs 22:6, NIV
Train a child in the way he should go, and when he is old he will not turn from it.

Proverbs 19:18
Discipline your son in his early years while there is hope. If you don't you will ruin his life.

Proverbs 13:24
If you refuse to discipline your son, it proves you don't love him; for if you love him you will be prompt to punish him.

Proverbs 22:15
A youngster's heart is filled with rebellion, but punishment will drive it out of him.

Ephesians 6:4
And now a word to you parents. Don't keep on scolding and nagging your children, making them angry and resentful. Rather, bring them up with the loving discipline the Lord himself approves, with suggestions and godly advice.

PROBLEM

Children may be disobedient and rebellious toward parents, guardians, or other authority figures.

BIBLICAL PERSPECTIVE

When a child is brought up according to scriptural principles, he will most likely continue to follow those principles later in life. Parents (or guardians) are responsible for the training and proper discipline of their children until such time as the children are no longer dependent upon them.

COUNSEL

Speak to the children on their own level of understanding. Make it clear to them what you expect of them. Do not punish them in anger. Set the example you want them to follow, remembering that what you do will be more effective than what you say. When you establish guidelines for children, stick to them. Take them with you to church and let them see you worship God and pray, then ask the Lord to show you what to do with them. Determine if there is a situation in the home that is directly contributing to the behavior problem of the children.

Father and mother, if both are in the family, must present a unified front:

- No parental disagreement in front of children.
- Don't be wishy-washy. Be specific in all instructions and discipline.

Recognize that parental responsibility extends over public school education, clubs, groups, and any other organization's influences upon your children.

While the child's attitudes belong to God, the parents or guardians must be faithful to their responsibility as outlined in the Bible. God will be faithful in changing the heart, but the parents must do their job.

Administer discipline according to the child's age and transgression. The rules of discipline are these:

- Establish clear guidelines so that your child knows what he is supposed to do and what he is not supposed to do.
- Punish disobedience.
- Discipline in love, not in anger.
- Make sure the child knows what he has done wrong.
- Demonstrate your love afterward.
- Always express forgiveness afterward, then treat the child as if it never happened.
- Follow through with discipline, making sure your commands are obeyed.
- If you make a mistake, apologize and ask forgiveness.

Remember, nothing will substitute for spending time with a child.

PRAYER

Make sure that the counselee knows Jesus; if not, minister salvation. Pray with the counselee and encourage him to join with you. Ask the Lord to help the counselee in his child discipline problem. Assure him that you and the other counselors will continue to pray for him.

READING

Dare to Discipline by James Dobson
The Strong-Willed Child by James Dobson

1 Timothy 3:4
He must have a well-behaved family, with children who obey quickly and quietly.

Titus 2:4
These older women must train the younger women to live quietly, to love their husbands and their children.

REFERENCES

Proverbs 13:24; 19:18; 22:15
Correction

Deuteronomy 4:9
Instruction

Proverbs 10:1; 8:32-36
Instruction

Ephesians 6:1-4
Instruction

2 Timothy 3:15
Instruction

_____

_____

_____

_____

_____

_____

_____

_____

_____

PROBLEM

The person needing help may be at a point either before or after completion of divorce proceedings. In either case a deeper commitment to God should be encouraged, but separate discussions and counseling apply.

BIBLICAL PERSPECTIVE

No problems are solved by lowering God's standards of lifelong marital fidelity (James 1:25). Satan, ever the destroyer, liar, thief, and deceiver, tries to convince some that problems will be resolved through marriage breakup (John 8:44; 1 Pet. 5:8).

SCRIPTURE

(Before)

Matthew 19:3b-9

"Do you permit divorce?" they asked.

"Don't you read the Scriptures?" he replied. "In them it is written that at the beginning God created man and woman, and that a man should leave his father and mother, and be forever united to his wife. The two shall become one—no longer two, but one! And no man may divorce what God has joined together."

"Then, why," they asked, "did Moses say a man may divorce his wife by merely writing her a letter of dismissal?"

Jesus replied, "Moses did that in recognition of your hard and evil hearts, but it was not what God had originally intended. And I tell you this, that anyone who divorces his wife, except for fornication, and marries another, commits adultery."

1 Corinthians 7:10-15

Now for those who are married I have a command, not just a suggestion. And it is not a command from me, for this is what the Lord himself has said: A wife must not leave her husband. But if she is separated from him, let her remain single or else go back to him. And the husband must not divorce his wife.

Here I want to add some suggestions of my own.

*These are not direct commands from the Lord, but
they seem right to me: if a Christian has a wife who is
not a Christian, but she wants to stay with him
anyway, he must not leave her or divorce her. And if a
Christian woman has a husband who isn't a Christian, and he wants her to stay with him, she must not
leave him. For perhaps the husband who isn't a
Christian may become a Christian with the help of his
Christian wife. And the wife who isn't a Christian
may become a Christian with the help of her Christian
husband. Otherwise, if the family separates, the
children might never come to know the Lord; whereas
a united family may, in God's plan, result in the
children's salvation.*

*But if the husband or wife who isn't a Christian is
eager to leave, it is permitted. In such cases the
Christian husband or wife should not insist that the
other stay, for God wants his children to live in peace
and harmony.*

(After)

II Peter 2:9 NIV (Repentance enjoined)
*The Lord is not slow in keeping His promises, as some
understand slowness. He is patient with you, not
wanting anyone to perish but everyone to come to
repentance.*

John 8:10, 11 (God forgives.)
*Then Jesus stood up again and said to her, "Where
are your accusers? Didn't even one of them condemn
you?"*

"No, sir," she said.

*And Jesus said, "Neither do I. Go and sin no
more."*

1 John 2:7-9 (Forgive the spouse.)
*Dear brothers, I am not writing out a new rule for
you to obey, for it is an old one you have always had,
right from the start. You have heard it all before. Yet it
is always new, and works for you just as it did for
Christ; and as we obey this commandment, to love
one another, the darkness in our lives disappears and
the new light of life in Christ shines in.*

*Anyone who says he is walking in the light of
Christ but dislikes his fellow man, is still in darkness.*

COUNSEL

(Before)

Try to determine the need for salvation in both partners. Help the counselee work toward the preservation of the marriage. He should be willing to consider taking one-sided steps toward reconciliation, even if the partner is involved in sin. In a marriage of a believer and an unbeliever, the choice of divorce should be left up to the unbeliever. If the unbeliever is the one who has asked for help, share Jesus. Remember that in some cases a believer may be helping to drive away the unbeliever, and thus committing sin. For either person asking whether divorce should be sought: it should be discouraged. Stress that the far-reaching consequences of divorce are too great to consider only oneself. Urge partners to consider their children: their futures and their present needs. Emphasize that sacrifices must be made. Stress belief that God will provide the love which can overrule all obstacles to oneness—including pride, self-seeking, self-serving, provoking one another. Urge both to forgive and learn to love one another. Pray with both parties. Encourage partners to seek fellowship and counsel in a local church that is Christ-centered and clearly teaches the Bible. (Also see the MARITAL RELATIONS section of the handbook.)

(After)

Determine the need for salvation in either party. Explain that divorce is not the unpardonable sin. Even to those who had been caught in sin, Jesus offered forgiveness and told them: "Go your way and sin no longer." A mistake may have been made, but one can go on with a renewed dedication to God. Stress the need for repentance (1 John 1:8, 9). The temptation to hate the divorced spouse must be discouraged.

Remind the counselee that God commands us to love one another. If no love exists in us, God can love through us. If we are open to the work of the Holy Spirit, he will stir up the love of Christ within us (Gal. 5:22, 23). What is needed is to start reorienting oneself (Rom. 12:2). If the counselee's present life-style has failed, it is time to acknowledge that God has a better plan. Anyone can begin to redirect his life toward God's love and God's will. (Other sections of the handbook may apply here, such as GUIDANCE, HOPE, FAITH, etc.)

PRAYER

Pray for God's leading as to how to pray for this person. Lead the counselee to ask God to forgive all those involved in the situation and to be open to healing of all hurts. Pray for the fruit of the Spirit to be produced in the counselee. Rebuke Satan for those attacked. Stand against him and with the counselee and the spouse. Above all, give praise to God.

FOLLOW-UP

For the spouse seeking reconciliation: List all the praiseworthy traits of your spouse. Share at least five each day with your spouse. Woo your spouse back. Also, take careful account of yourself. Seek counsel on how to improve yourself as needed, such as in habits, appearance, mannerisms, etc. Don't just tell your spouse how you are going to change; show him or her by changing yourself.

READING
Divorce by John Murray
The Christian Family by Larry Christenson
Prison to Praise and other books by Merlin Carothers

REFERENCES

1 Corinthians 13
Love

Galatians 5
Flesh and spirit

John 15
Sticking to Jesus

Hebrews 11
Faith

Ephesians 5
Duty to spouses

Colossians 3
Duty to spouses

1 Corinthians 7
The marriage bond

SCRIPTURE

Proverbs 18:22
The man who finds a wife finds a good thing; she is a blessing to him from the Lord.

1 Timothy 5:14
So I think it is better for these younger widows to marry again and have children, and take care of their own homes; then no one will be able to say anything against them.

Hebrews 13:4
Honor your marriage and its vows, and be pure; for God will surely punish all those who are immoral or commit adultery.

Matthew 5:32
But I say that a man who divorces his wife, except for fornication, causes her to commit adultery if she marries again. And he who marries her commits adultery.

Mark 10:9
And no man may separate what God has joined together.

1 Corinthians 7:3, 4
The man should give his wife all that is her right as a married woman, and the wife should do the same for her husband: for a girl who marries no longer has full right to her own body, for her husband then has his rights to it, too, and in the same way the husband no longer has full right to his own body, for it belongs also to his wife.

PROBLEM

The person's marriage may be on the verge of breaking up; separation may have already occurred. In marital conflict, disagreement and mistrust are the rule rather than the exception.

BIBLICAL PERSPECTIVE

The scriptural ideal is that two shall become one flesh (Gen. 2:24). God intended the man and the woman to be bound together until death (Rom. 7:2; 1 Cor. 7:10, 11; Mark 10:9).

COUNSEL

Try to find the root cause of the marital conflict, i.e., inability to accept the other person as he is, unforgiveness, lack of submission to the other, etc. Intercede on behalf of the couple, praising God for what he will do. Denounce Satan (Matt. 18:18). He is a liar and a deceiver and desires to destroy marriages.

Pray for God's grace on the persons involved (Ps. 103:8). The Lord desires to shine his face upon them and be gracious to them (Num. 6:4-6). He wants to ground them and plant their roots deep. He is keeping them according to his power working in them (Eph. 3:17-20).

Therefore, at each encouragement, praise God for restoring and blessing the marriage (Heb. 13:15).

If a person chooses to fast in behalf of the people involved, interceding in prayer and standing for the spiritually weak partners, God has promised to honor such a fast and repair the breach (Isa. 58:6-12).

Do not take sides yourself, creating a three-way conflict.

Refer the person(s) to a pastor for counseling at a Christ-centered church that clearly teaches the Bible.

PRAYER
Offer thanks and praise to God for working out
the rough places and giving hope and renewal.

REFERENCES

Duties of husbands and wives:
Genesis 2:23, 24
Proverbs 5:18
Proverbs 31
Ecclesiastes 9:9
1 Corinthians 7:10
Ephesians 5:22, 25
1 Peter 3:1, 7
1 Timothy 3:11

FOLLOW-UP
Make a list of all the things for which you can
honestly praise your spouse. Each day share five
of these, instead of criticizing, for at least one
week. Continue until your list runs out.

READING
Divorce by John Murray
The Christian Family by Larry Christenson
Favor: The Road to Success by Bob Buess

SCRIPTURE

Deuteronomy 12:28
Be careful to obey all of these commandments. If you do what is right in the eyes of the Lord your God, all will go well with you and your children forever.

Colossians 3:20
You children must always obey your fathers and mothers, for that pleases the Lord.

Ephesians 6:1-4
Children, obey your parents: this is the right thing to do because God has placed them in authority over you. Honor your father and mother. This is the first of God's Ten Commandments that ends with a promise. And this is the promise: that if you honor your father and mother, yours will be a long life, full of blessing. And now a word to you parents. Don't keep on scolding and nagging your children, making them angry and resentful. Rather, bring them up with the loving discipline the Lord approves, with suggestions and godly advice.

_____

_____

_____

_____

PROBLEM

Family relationships are often marred by conflict, rebellion, lack of discipline, confusion, and anxiety. The counselee is seeking to restore family relationships and peace in the home.

BIBLICAL PERSPECTIVE

Growth in the Christian life requires discipline of self and submitting oneself to others. In the case of children, the submission is first to the parents. Children are always to honor and obey parents in the Lord (Eph. 5 and 6).

COUNSEL

Emphasize the need to manifest the fruit of the Spirit (Gal. 5:22, 23). These qualities are needed in order for the counselee to be the prime motivator in the family. As the fruit of the Spirit become more evident through spiritual maturity, he will find himself more and more able to administer discipline, love, and order in the home.

The promise of Acts 16:31 is written to parents. Parents need to receive the assurance that this promise will be fulfilled.

If the counselee is a child in the home, emphasize the necessity of obeying the parents, since to disobey one's parents is to disobey God and bring disorder and confusion into the home.

Emphasize the need for a renewing of the mind. As with counselees who are parents, start with studying the references to the fruit of the Spirit. Talk through Scripture references regarding parent-child relationships. Emphasize the need for giving God preeminence in all matters and all relationships.

PRAYER

Pray for the counselee and his family. Pray for the Holy Spirit to give the counselee discernment about the problem areas in his family. Ask God to reveal to him his part in bringing about a victorious solution to his family concerns.

REFERENCES

1 Corinthians 11:1-12; Ephesians 5:22–6:4; Colossians 3:16-21
Divine order in the home

Philemon
Relationships restored in Christ

Isaiah 58
Fasting to restore relationships

Proverbs 13:24; 29:15; 19:18; Hebrews 12:5-11
Guidance for parents

Ephesians 6:1-3; Colossians 3:20
Guidance for children

READING

The Christian Family by Larry Christenson
Seven Styles of Parenting by Pat Hershey Owen
The Strong-Willed Child by James Dobson
Dare to Discipline by James Dobson

SCRIPTURE

1 Corinthians 7:15, KJV
But if the unbelieving depart, let him depart. A brother or a sister is not under bondage in such cases: but God hath called us to peace.

1 Corinthians 7:27, 28a, KJV
Art thou bound unto a wife? seek not to be loosed. Art thou loosed from a wife? seek not a wife. But if thou marry, thou hast not sinned.

Matthew 19:9
And I tell you this, that anyone who divorces his wife, except for fornication, and marries another, commits adultery.

1 Corinthians 7:39
The wife is part of her husband as long as he lives; if her husband dies, then she may marry again, but only if she marries a Christian.

PROBLEM

Remarriage is a very sensitive and difficult issue to resolve within the church. The very issue of remarriage says there has been a divorce, except when a spouse has died. The church is somewhat divided on the permissive will of God concerning divorce and remarriage.

BIBLICAL PERSPECTIVE

It is very clear that God's Word does permit remarriage when a spouse dies. In the case where adultery has been committed by the other partner the Word does permit remarriage. It also appears that in the case of desertion by an unbelieving spouse there is freedom for the believer to remarry; however, remarriages other than on these grounds are discouraged. God's perfect will is for reconciliation rather than divorce/remarriage (see 1 Cor. 7:10, 11).

COUNSEL

When a marriage has dissolved, for whatever reason—desertion, adultery—every effort should be made to restore the relationship. It seems that our primary difficulty in interpersonal relationships is in the area of forgiving one another even when we are exhorted strongly through Scripture to forgive in order to be forgiven (see Matt. 6:14, 15).

The Word discourages remarriage in 1 Corinthians 7:32-35. "I am saying this to help you, not to try to keep you from marrying. I want you to do whatever will help you serve the Lord best, with as few other things as possible to distract your attention from him."

These words should be pondered carefully whenever remarriage is being considered. Each case is unique, and in every circumstance a person should move slowly, pray earnestly, and seek godly counsel.

In regard to divorces and remarriages that have occurred before becoming a Christian, it seems clear that all such things are part of the old life that has been left behind (see 2 Cor. 5:17). In other words, if a person was married, divorced, and then remarried, and then is born again in the midst of the second marriage, they should not divorce their present spouse to return to the first.

All remarriage plans other than those on the permissive scriptural grounds previously stated must be dealt with as sin and confessed and repented of (see 1 John 1:9).

Sound biblical counsel should be sought from a Christ-centered, Bible-believing pastor or counselor before any final remarriage plans are made.

When the Lord grants his approval to the remarriage plans, then both parties are scripturally bound and accountable to all of God's Word concerning marriage. (See the section on MARITAL RELATIONS.)

PRAYER

Encourage the counselee contemplating remarriage to confess and repent of any part he may have had in the failure of his previous marriage. He must also deal with any guilt, resentment, bitterness, or unforgiveness from his past marriage. He must pray and ask God to set him free from the past and to give him clear direction for his new marriage.

READING

The Christian Family by Larry Christenson

REFERENCES

1 Corinthians 7:2, 8, 9
Let every man have his own wife; let every woman have her own husband

1 Timothy 5:14
Younger widows to marry

1 Corinthians 13
Love in action

Ephesians 5
Duty to spouses

Colossians 3
Duty to spouses

1 Corinthians 7
The marriage bond

1 Peter 3:1-7
Responsibilities of spouses

FINANCES

SCRIPTURE

Matthew 6:33
And he will give them to you if you give him first place in your life and live as he wants you to.

Malachi 3:8-10
Will a man rob God? Surely not! And yet you have robbed me.

Philippians 4:18, 19
At the moment I have all I need—more than I need! I am generously supplied with the gifts you sent me when Epaphroditus came. They are a sweet-smelling sacrifice that pleases God well. And it is he who will supply all your needs from his riches in glory, because of what Christ Jesus has done for us.

_____
_____
_____
_____
_____
_____
_____
_____
_____
_____
_____
_____
_____

PROBLEM

Many persons face the inability to meet financial obligations. This can be brought on by family emergencies (such as extended medical treatment), bad investments, gambling, birth of a child, taking in relatives or friends, and so forth.

BIBLICAL PERSPECTIVE

God has promised to meet all of his children's needs if they are living according to his will (Matt. 6:31-33). Believers who are faithful in their tithing and giving of offerings are promised an abundance of blessing (Mal. 3:8-10).

COUNSEL

If the counselee is a Christian who seems to be living a righteous life (including the giving of tithes and offerings) but is still experiencing financial problems, offer assurance that God is true to his promises and that he will provide for our needs. The Bible assures us that we will reap in due time if we don't faint along the way. Encourage the counselee to expect God's providential care. Also, God may be using the times of financial trouble to reorient the person in his vocation and life-style. Times of financial difficulty may be times when the person should reconsider his priorities and his previous habits of giving, spending, and investing.

Fasting may be needed to loose yokes and break bonds. See Isaiah 58:6-8.

PRAYER

Offer thanks and praise to God for the gifts he has already bestowed upon the counselee. Pray for patience while the person awaits the fulfillment of God's promises. Pray that the time of difficulty will be a time of blessing as the person grows in his understanding of how to properly use the material benefits God bestows.

REFERENCES

Luke 6:38
Give and you shall receive

Proverbs 21:20
Admonition to save

Proverbs 24:3, 4
Developing a profitable business

Proverbs 28:22
Get-rich-quick schemes lead nowhere

Psalm 37:4, 5
God will give us our heart's desires

2 Corinthians 9:6-9
We reap as we plant

READING

Your Money: Frustration or Freedom by Howard L. Dayton, Jr.
How to Live Like a King's Kid by Harold Hill
Money Matters by R. C. Sproul, Jr.
Principles under Scrutiny by Larry Burkett

SCRIPTURE

Proverbs 19:17
When you help the poor you are lending to the Lord—and he pays wonderful interest on your loan!

Malachi 3:8-11
"Will a man rob God? Surely not! And yet you have robbed me."

"What do you mean? When did we ever rob you?"

"You have robbed me of the tithes and offerings due to me. And so the awesome curse of God is cursing you, for your whole nation has been robbing me. Bring all the tithes into the storehouse so that there will be food enough in my Temple; if you do, I will open up the windows of heaven for you and pour out a blessing so great you won't have room enough to take it in!

"Try it! Let me prove it to you! Your crops will be large, for I will guard them from insects and plagues. Your grapes won't shrivel away before they ripen, says the Lord Almighty."

Luke 6:38
For if you give, you will get! Your gift will return to you in full and overflowing measure, pressed down, shaken together to make room for more, and running over. Whatever measure you use to give—large or small—will be used to measure what is given back to you.

DESCRIPTION

To give means to be committed to the stewardship of one's possessions for God. To tithe is to present a tenth of our prosperity to God—whether money, objects of value, or talents and time.

BIBLICAL PERSPECTIVE

Both the Old and New Testaments speak of the stewardship of our material wealth. We are to give freely of that which we have received; we are responsible for the right use of all our gifts. Tithes and offerings are an example of giving. The poor and otherwise needy around us are to be the special recipients of what we have to give (Deut. 15:11; Prov. 3:9, 10).

COUNSEL

The Jews were required to tithe by law. Christians today should be expected to do no less—to tithe and give an offering under God's grace. If the counselee is inquiring about whether to tithe or give certain amounts, encourage him to study the Scriptures cited and even to try tithing for six months. If he is to be convinced to tithe, the Spirit will convict him. The tithe and offering should be given as the Holy Spirit leads.

Remember that an offering is given after the tithe. Giving is to be done willingly, regardless of the amount given.

We are also to give to the broader Church (all the body of Christ). This support is much further reaching. (See 1 Cor. 16:1, 2.) Therefore, we find ourselves with many avenues open to our giving.

If a person has no particular local congregation, refer him to one. He must decide how he is to account for this stewardship of tithes and offerings, as the Spirit leads.

PRAYER

Lead the counselee to offer a prayer of commitment to tithe and give offerings.

REFERENCES

Malachi 3:8-11
Tithing and robbing God

Matthew 22:15-22
Render to Caesar his own

Luke 6:38
Give and receive good measure

1 Corinthians 16:1, 2
Giving to needy saints

_____

_____

_____

_____

_____

_____

_____

_____

_____

_____

_____

_____

_____

_____

_____

_____

Matthew 6:1
Take care! Don't do your good deeds publicly, to be admired, for then you will lose the reward from your Father in heaven.

2 Corinthians 9:6-12
But remember this—if you give little, you will get little. A farmer who plants just a few seeds will get only a small crop, but if he plants much, he will reap much. Every one must make up his own mind as to how much he should give. Don't force anyone to give more than he really wants to, for cheerful givers are the ones God prizes. God is able to make it up to you by giving you everything you need and more, so that there will not only be enough for your own needs, but plenty left over to give joyfully to others. It is as the Scriptures say: "The godly man gives generously to the poor. His good deeds will be an honor to him forever." . . .

Yes, God will give you much so that you can give away much, and when we take your gifts to those who need them they will break out into thanksgiving and praise to God for your help. So, two good things happen as a result of your gifts—those in need are helped, and they overflow with thanks to God.

GOD'S GIFTS

SCRIPTURE

Genesis 15:6
And Abram believed God; then God considered him righteous on account of his faith.

John 3:16
For God loved the world so much that he gave his only Son so that anyone who believes in him shall not perish but have eternal life.

Romans 1:17
This Good News tells us that God makes us ready for heaven—makes us right in God's sight—when we put our faith and trust in Christ to save us. This is accomplished from start to finish by faith. As the Scripture says it, "The man who finds life will find it through trusting God."

————————————

————————————

————————————

————————————

————————————

————————————

————————————

————————————

————————————

————————————

————————————

PROBLEM

We all have faith in something. It may be in self, money, heritage, family, a religious system, etc. But unless our faith is in God and is growing, we have an unfulfilled life on earth and no hope of heaven.

BIBLICAL PERSPECTIVE

God requires that we have faith in him and he even gives us that faith (Heb. 11:6; Rom. 10:17).

COUNSEL

Tell the counselee that faith is necessary in the Christian life:

To be made right with God and to have peace (Rom. 1:17; 5:1).
To receive eternal life (John 3:16; Eph. 2:8, 9).
To be assured that our prayers will be answered (Matt. 17:20; James 1:5-8).
To please God (Heb. 11:6).

Faith comes from God:

God gives each person a certain amount of faith (Rom. 12:3).
God gives some Christians the gift of extraordinary faith (1 Cor. 12:9).
God gives more faith to those who listen to the Good News about Jesus Christ (Rom. 10:17).

PRAYER

Pray that God will increase the counselee's faith as he studies the faith-building Word and exercises the faith he already has.

REFERENCES

John 5:24
Faith gives the assurance of eternal life

John 12:46
Faith will keep us from wandering in darkness

John 20:31
Faith in Christ comes from reading God's Word

Romans 10:9, 10
Faith brings salvation

Ephesians 6:16
Faith stops the fiery arrows aimed at us by Satan

Hebrews 11
Faith chapter of the Bible

_____
_____
_____
_____
_____
_____
_____
_____
_____
_____
_____
_____
_____
_____
_____
_____

Romans 5:1
So now, since we have been made right in God's sight by faith in his promises, we can have real peace with him because of what Jesus Christ our Lord has done for us.

Romans 10:17
Yet faith comes from listening to this Good News—the Good News about Christ.

Ephesians 2:8, 9
Because of his kindness you have been saved through trusting Christ. And even trusting is not of yourselves, it too is a gift from God. Salvation is not a reward for the good we have done, so none of us can take any credit for it.

Hebrews 11:1, 6
What is faith? It is the confident assurance that something we want is going to happen. It is the certainty that what we hope for is waiting for us, even though we cannot see it up ahead.
You can never please God without faith, without depending on him. Anyone who wants to come to God must believe that there is a God and that he rewards those who sincerely look for him.

SCRIPTURE

Matthew 7:16, 20
You can detect them by the way they act, just as you can identify a tree by its fruit. You need never confuse grapevines with thorn bushes or figs with thistles.

Yes, the way to identify a tree or a person is by the kind of fruit produced.

John 15:4, 5
Take care to live in me, and let me live in you. For a branch can't produce fruit when severed from the vine. Nor can you be fruitful apart from me.

Yes, I am the Vine; you are the branches. Whoever lives in me and I in him shall produce a large crop of fruit. For apart from me you can't do a thing.

Galatians 5:22, 23
But when the Holy Spirit controls our lives he will produce this kind of fruit in us: love, joy, peace, patience, kindness, goodness, faithfulness, gentleness and self-control; and here there is no conflict with Jewish laws.

PROBLEM

Those who follow their own wrong inclinations will find that their lives produce such evil results as:

eagerness for lustful pleasure
idolatry
spiritism
hatred
fighting
jealousy
anger
selfish ambition
complaining
criticism
feeling that everyone else is wrong except those in their own small group
wrong doctrine
envy
murder
drunkenness
wild parties

BIBLICAL PERSPECTIVE

Our yielding to the flesh will produce all kinds of evil results (Gal. 5:19-21), but when the Holy Spirit controls our lives he will produce the kind of fruit that is pleasing to God (Gal. 5:22, 23).

COUNSEL

How to have the fruit of the Spirit in abundance:

Become a Christian. The Holy Spirit is none other than the Spirit of Jesus Christ himself. So, in order to have the fruit of the Spirit, we must first invite Jesus Christ to live in us. Paul wrote, "If anyone doesn't have the Spirit of Christ living in him, he is not a Christian at all" (Rom. 8:9); "When someone becomes a Christian he becomes a brand new person inside. He is not the same any more. A new life has begun" (2 Cor. 5:17). The Holy Spirit will produce his fruit in the life of a Christian who desires to grow in spiritual maturity.

Be filled with the Holy Spirit. It is never hard to tell when a person is under the control of an alcoholic beverage; he acts like it. With that logic in mind, Paul wrote, "Be filled instead with the Holy Spirit, and controlled by him" (Eph. 5:18). So if Paul says "be filled," it must be both possible and a choice we are to make.

Just as the Father will "give the Holy Spirit to those who ask him" (Luke 11:13), so we can be sure that he is also wanting to see the fruit of the Spirit abundantly produced in all of his children.

When we allow the Holy Spirit to control our lives, the fruit of the Spirit that brings glory to God is then manifested (Gal. 5:22, 23).

Follow the Holy Spirit's leading. The Holy Spirit will continue to produce fruit as we carefully follow his leading in every part of our lives (Gal. 5:25). To "follow his leading" simply means that we cooperate with the work of the Holy Spirit in us and obey the known will of God. Then the Holy Spirit will produce in us an abundance of "love, joy, peace, patience, kindness, goodness, faithfulness, gentleness and self-control" (Gal. 5:22, 23).

PRAYER

Pray with the counselee that God will specifically point to any unconfessed sins and cleanse his heart with the blood of Christ. Pray that he will fill the counselee with his Holy Spirit and teach him to follow his leading so that others will see the fruit of the Spirit and praise our heavenly Father (Matt. 5:16).

FOLLOW-UP

Study the following Scriptures. Each one refers to a fruit of the Spirit God wants to produce in our lives.

Love
Luke 10:25-27; 1 Corinthians 13; 1 John 3:10, 11, 18, 19

Joy
John 15:11; 16:24

Peace
Isaiah 26:3; John 14:27

Patience
Romans 5:3

Kindness
1 Corinthians 13:4; 2 Corinthians 6:6; Colossians 3:12

Goodness
Ephesians 5:9

Faithfulness
1 Corinthians 4:2

Gentleness
Galatians 6:1; 1 Timothy 6:11; Titus 3:2; 1 Peter 3:15

Self-control
Acts 24:25; 2 Peter 1:6

_____
_____
_____
_____
_____

SCRIPTURE

1 Corinthians 12:7-11
The Holy Spirit displays God's power through each of us as a means of helping the entire church.

To one person the Spirit gives the ability to give wise advice; someone else may be especially good at studying and teaching, and this is his gift from the same Spirit. He gives special faith to another, and to someone else the power to heal the sick. He gives power for doing miracles to some, and to others power to prophesy and preach. He gives someone else the power to know whether evil spirits are speaking through those who claim to be giving God's messages—or whether it is really the Spirit of God who is speaking. Still another person is able to speak in languages he never learned; and others, who do not know the language either, are given power to understand what he is saying. It is the same and only Holy Spirit who gives all these gifts and powers, deciding which each one of us should have.

DESCRIPTION

Charis is a Greek word meaning "grace." *Charismata* is Greek for "gifts of grace." A gift is a Spirit-given ability for Christian service. The Holy Spirit is both gift and giver. The word *charismatic* describes those Christians who believe in the manifestation of the gifts *(charismata)* of the Holy Spirit.

BIBLICAL PERSPECTIVE

The gifts of the Spirit are supernatural endowments for service and are given according to the nature of the ministry that is to be fulfilled. The purpose of all the gifts is the same: to edify the body. We should first seek Jesus, the Giver of the Spirit. The disciples waited for the promise of the Father, the Holy Spirit—not for gifts (Acts 1). Thus we are to set our own hearts on him, for he gives the gifts as he chooses.

COUNSEL

Paul encouraged his readers to abound in the things of the Lord. "Give him first place in your life and live as he wants you to" (Matt. 6:33). Then the appropriate gifts will automatically be given, as they are needed for ministry.

There is a tendency to regard gifts as measures of spirituality. The Bible says we are known by our fruits, not our gifts (Gal. 5:22, 23). Fruit (virtues or qualities of the Spirit) is available to all Christians; gifts are given differently to individual Christians for the good of all.

Tongues is the most problematical of the gifts. For those who object to tongues, refer them to 1 Corinthians 14:39, 40. For those who seem to be abusive of the gift, refer them to 1 Corinthians 14:19.

PRAYER

The counselee who is seeking a gift or gifts must pray to the Giver in faith, believing. First we receive the Giver, and then it follows that we should be able to openly receive the gifts. Pray that the counselee will use the gifts in love to benefit the body of Christ. Pray that, having given the person gifts, God will then put him in a place of service where he can use them.

REFERENCES

1 Corinthians 12
Gifts listed

Romans 12:3-8
Using the gifts (cf. 1 Pet. 4:10, 11)

Ephesians 4:11
Offices in which gifts are used

_____
_____
_____
_____
_____
_____
_____
_____
_____
_____
_____
_____
_____
_____

Ephesians 4:11-13
Some of us have been given special ability as apostles; to others he has given the gift of being able to preach well; some have special ability in winning people to Christ, helping them to trust him as their Savior; still others have a gift for caring for God's people as a shepherd does his sheep, leading and teaching them in the ways of God.

Why is it that he gives us these special abilities to do certain things best? It is that God's people will be equipped to do better work for him, building up the Church, the body of Christ, to a position of strength and maturity; until finally we all believe alike about our salvation and about our Savior, God's Son, and all become full-grown in the Lord—yes, to the point of being filled full with Christ.

1 Peter 4:10, 11
God has given each of you some special abilities; be sure to use them to help each other, passing on to others God's many kinds of blessings. Are you called to preach? Then preach as though God himself were speaking through you. Are you called to help others? Do it with all the strength and energy that God supplies, so that God will be glorified through Jesus Christ—to him be glory and power forever and ever. Amen.

SCRIPTURE

Acts 1:5
"John baptized you with water," he reminded them, "but you shall be baptized with the Holy Spirit in just a few days."

Acts 1:8
But when the Holy Spirit has come upon you, you will receive power to testify about me with great effect, to the people in Jerusalem, throughout Judea, in Samaria, and to the ends of the earth, about my death and resurrection.

Acts 2:4
And everyone present was filled with the Holy Spirit and began speaking languages they didn't know, for the Holy Spirit gave them this ability.

Acts 2:16-18
No! What you see this morning was predicted centuries ago by the prophet Joel—"In the last days," God said, "I will pour out my Holy Spirit upon all mankind, and your sons and daughters shall prophesy, and your young men shall see visions, and your old men dream dreams. Yes, the Holy Spirit shall come upon all my servants, men and women alike, and they shall prophesy."

DESCRIPTION

A desire for blessing from the Holy Spirit and a renewed relationship with God through this experience.

BIBLICAL PERSPECTIVE

Baptism in the Holy Spirit is the overflowing of the Spirit into, upon, and out of a born-again believer. It is the fulfillment of the promise the Father gave to all believers. Its purpose is to lead to a full, meaningful, and rewarding life in Jesus Christ (Joel 2:28-30; Acts 2:16-18).

COUNSEL

Jesus is the one who baptizes with the Holy Spirit. When you pray for the Holy Spirit to come in blessing, ask the Father as Jesus said to in Luke 11:13. Just as people have experienced since the Day of Pentecost (Acts 2), the person prayed for will receive the Holy Spirit in power and strength.

Ask God to anoint the counselee once he has asked for the baptism and is before the Lord in worship. Then in quiet praise and prayer with the person, wait for the anointing, the witness, and the evidence of a praise language to come forth.

Salvation is the qualification to receive the baptism in the Spirit. Speaking in unlearned languages is a gift from God for one's own edification (1 Cor. 14:2, 4), to extol the works of God (Acts 2:11), and to present a message from God (1 Cor. 12:10; 14:6).

Encourage the counselee to worship in a Christ-centered church that clearly teaches the Bible, and to start growing in understanding, experience, wisdom, and knowledge.

PRAYER

Lead the counselee to thank God for baptizing him with the Spirit. Offer thanksgiving and praise along with him for this gift. As you are praising God, you should expect him to reveal further needs of the counselee, such as healing for himself, his family or relatives, or other needs.

REFERENCES

Joel 2:28-30
Prophecy

Acts 2:16-18
Prophecy

John 14; 16
Promised by Jesus

Acts 1:5-8
Promised by Jesus

Acts 2
Fulfillment

Acts 2:1-11
Evidence

Acts 10:44-48
At salvation

Acts 19:1-7
After salvation

1 Corinthians 14:4
Tongues of edification

Isaiah 28:11, 12
For rest in the Lord

READING

They Speak with Other Tongues by John Sherrill
Nine O'Clock in the Morning by Dennis Bennett
"That's the Spirit," tract from CBN

Acts 2:38
And Peter replied, "Each one of you must turn from sin, return to God, and be baptized in the name of Jesus Christ for the forgiveness of your sins; then you also shall receive this gift, the Holy Spirit."

Luke 11:13
And if even sinful persons like yourselves give children what they need, don't you realize that your heavenly Father will do at least as much and give the Holy Spirit to those who ask for him?

_____

_____

_____

_____

_____

_____

_____

_____

_____

_____

_____

_____

_____

_____

SCRIPTURE

Romans 8:24
We are saved by trusting. And trusting means looking forward to getting something we don't yet have—for a man who already has something doesn't need to hope and trust that he will get it.

Acts 10:43
And all the prophets have written about him, saying that everyone who believes in him will have their sins forgiven through his name.

John 14:27
I am leaving you with a gift— peace of mind and heart! And the peace I give isn't fragile like the peace the world gives. So don't be troubled or afraid.

1 John 1:3
Again I say, we are telling you about what we ourselves have actually seen and heard, so that you may share the fellowship and the joys we have with the Father and with Jesus Christ his Son.

Matthew 11:28-30
Come to me and I will give you rest—all of you who work so hard beneath a heavy yoke. Wear my yoke—for it fits perfectly—and let me teach you; for I am gentle and humble, and you shall find rest for your soul; for I give you only light burdens.

PROBLEM

A need for hope (desire combined with expectation) is often characterized by anguish, despair, and hopelessness in the person seeking help.

BIBLICAL PERSPECTIVE

Every promise in the Bible, God says, is meant especially for Christians. The Christian has favor with God. He will see to it that those who walk in his favor will find favor with other people.

COUNSEL

The above promises are made by God specifically to the Christian. Help the counselee to be familiar with the hope God offers in Christ, which is sometimes expressed as "treasure in heaven" (Matt. 19:21) or "living water" (John 4:1-15). Help him to expand his vision to include what God can and desires to do in his life, to bring hope and a future of fulfillment.

PRAYER

Thank God that in spite of problems, we can maintain hope. A declaration of our hope as recorded in 2 Corinthians 4:7-9 would be appropriate.

Counselor: The person seeking hope needs faith to be built up as well, and for his mind to be renewed. Ask the Lord for insight into the underlying cause of the anxiety and lack of hope.

REFERENCES

Romans 5:1-5
How hope is gained

Romans 4:18-25
The faith of Abraham

Psalm 23
God's assurances

2 Corinthians 4:7; 5:8
Reflect God's grace; do not fear death

Isaiah 50:10
The answer to fear and darkness

PROBLEM

The counselee may have a strong ego and pride that is getting in the way of a proper relationship with God and others. The opposite of pride is humility, which involves being realistic about one's vulnerability and looking upon oneself as a servant of others. A humble person does not feel or act superior and does not show favoritism in his dealings with others.

BIBLICAL PERSPECTIVE

Pride is continually condemned in both Old and New Testaments. Man is God's creature and has no right to lord it over other persons, since God alone is over man. Christ, Moses, and many other admirable characters in the Bible are portrayed as humble men who acted as servants, not arrogant lords. Those who exalt themselves will, according to Scripture, be humbled while the humble will be exalted. The person who would be first should make himself servant of all, for the last shall be first and the first shall be last (Matt. 20:16).

COUNSEL

Many people do not realize that much of their behavior is the result of being on an ego trip. Pride is part of our natural sin of self-centered-ness. Almost every problem we experience can be traced to it, and it can be taken to such extremes that the person may actually worship himself, as evidenced by his total devotion to his own interests.

SCRIPTURE

James 4:10
Then when you realize your worthlessness before the Lord, he will lift you up, encourage and help you.

Mark 10:45
For even I, the Messiah, am not here to be served, but to help others, and to give my life as a ransom for many.

Proverbs 18:12
Pride ends in destruction; humility ends in honor.

Proverbs 16:18
Pride goes before destruction and haughtiness before a fall.

Micah 6:8
No, he has told you what he wants, and this is all it is: to be fair and just and merciful, and to walk humbly with your God.

_____

_____

_____

_____

_____

_____

_____

_____

126

REFERENCES

James 4:6
Humility is rewarded

Philippians 2:5-11
Christ as an example of
humility

Matthew 16:24
Denying oneself

Isaiah 57:15; 66:2
The humble dwell with God

Luke 14:11
Humility brings greatness

Romans 12:3
Admonition to humility

Matthew 11:29
Christ as an example of
meekness

READING
The Inflated Self by David
G. Myers

—————————————
—————————————
—————————————
—————————————
—————————————
—————————————
—————————————

Pride is not always noticeable, for many egotistical people manage to conceal their pride and self-centeredness. However, a proud person often talks down to people and assumes a discernible air of superiority.

Our natural state—because of the Fall—is one of self-centeredness and pride. But a fruit of the Spirit is meekness, and one aspect of meekness is humility.

In talking with the counselee, determine whether there is a need to make a commitment to Christ. In working to lead the person to Christ, make him aware that part of the cost of giving oneself to God is surrendering the ego as the center of one's life. The person who is saved knows that Christ, and Christ alone, is to be at the center of existence.

If the counselee is already a Christian, he may simply need to be reminded that the model for the Christian life is Christ, who made it clear that humility, not pride, is the proper course for disciples. The Scriptures in this section should help the person gain a proper perspective on the need for humility.

PRAYER
Pray that the fruit of the Spirit will be manifested in the counselee. Pray that God will keep the person mindful of human vulnerability and the need to act as a servant to fellow human beings.

PROBLEM
Love is essential to any relationship, yet many lack the quality of love God requires. We all need to grow in our love for God and for people.

BIBLICAL PERSPECTIVE
God commands us to love him and people (Luke 10:25-37). In fact, if we do not love people, it is evident we do not love God (1 John 3:10, 11, 18, 19).

COUNSEL
We love because God commands us to. Jesus commands us to love God and our neighbor (Mark 12:29-31). It is possible and it must be a deliberate act of our will to love as Jesus loves. The love God wants us to have is not merely an emotional feeling which may come and go, but a volitional love which is based on a decision and a commitment, and cannot be destroyed by circumstances.

We love in response to God's love. We are able to love God because he first loved us (1 John 4:19), and we love others because of the loving relationship God has begun with us (1 John 3:10, 11, 17, 18).

We are to love all kinds of people. The Bible teaches that our love is to include all people; our spouse (Eph. 5:25; Titus 2:4), neighbors (Luke 10:27-37), other Christians (1 Pet. 2:17), and even enemies (Matt. 5:43).

Our love is to be practical. If we love God, we will obey him (John 14:24). If we love people, we will act like it (1 Cor. 13), and show it in material ways (1 John 3:17, 18).

SCRIPTURE
Mark 12:29-31
Jesus replied, "The one that says, 'Hear, O Israel! The Lord our God is the one and only God. And you must love him with all your heart and soul and mind and strength.'

"The second is: 'You must love others as much as yourself.' No other commandments are greater than these."

1 John 4:19-21
So you see, our love for him comes as a result of his loving us first. If anyone says, "I love God," but keeps on hating his brother, he is a liar; for if he doesn't love his brother who is right there in front of him, how can he love God whom he has never seen? And God himself has said that one must love not only God, but his brother too.

128

---

1 Corinthians 13:4-7, 13

Love is very patient and kind, never jealous or envious, never boastful or proud, never haughty or selfish or rude. Love does not demand its own way. It is not irritable or touchy. It does not hold grudges and will hardly even notice when others do it wrong. It is never glad about injustice, but rejoices whenever truth wins out. If you love someone you will be loyal to him no matter what the cost. You will always believe in him, always expect the best of him, and always stand your ground in defending him.

There are three things that remain—faith, hope, and love—and the greatest of these is love.

_____

_____

_____

_____

_____

_____

_____

_____

_____

_____

Many Christians have adopted a nonbiblical view of love. We must become acquainted with what the Bible teaches about love and be convinced that it is true, then practice it as an act of obedience. God set the example when he showed his love for us at a time when we certainly didn't deserve it (Rom. 5:6-8).

Show love, even to those you don't think deserve it; the joy of God's love will fill your heart as you prayerfully obey the Lord.

PRAYER

Pray that God will give the counselee the will to love and show love to others. Have him pray that each day his love for God will grow and be increasingly evident to others.

REFERENCES

John 3:16; Ephesians 2:4, 5
God's love for the world

Matthew 22:37, 38; John 13:34
Love God and your neighbor

FOLLOW-UP

Think of a person you find difficult to love. Plan to do special favors for that person until you know that God has finally been able to plant his love in your heart. Then choose another person and do the same. Obediently and sacrificially show love and God will take care of your feelings. Eventually it will feel quite natural, regardless of whether or not the person you are loving deserves it.

Study the Scriptures referred to in this section.

PROBLEM

There are many who suffer from inner turmoil, often resulting in observable nervous tension, irrational behavior, insomnia, fatigue, and strained relationships. They need peace of mind.

BIBLICAL PERSPECTIVE

God is the One who gives peace (Isa. 26:3). Jesus, the Prince of Peace (Isa. 9:6), told his disciples that he would give them peace (John 14:27). When the Holy Spirit controls our lives, he produces peace in us (Gal. 5:22).

COUNSEL

Six Steps to Inner Peace

Be made right with God. The one who has placed his faith in Jesus Christ is made right with God and can, for the first time, have real peace (Rom. 5:1).

Let the peace of Christ always be present in your heart. Peace of heart comes from Christ (Col. 3:15). So, when we give Christ first place in our life and live as he wants us to (Matt. 6:33), he gives us peace of heart. As members of the body of Christ, this is our responsibility and privilege (Col. 3:15).

Fix your thoughts on the Lord and what is good. Those who trust in the Lord and turn their thoughts often to him will have perfect peace (Isa. 26:3). And the God of peace promises to be with those who fix their thoughts on what is true and good and right, and on those things they can praise God for (Phil. 4:8, 9).

Confess your sins to God. One method God uses to keep us pure and in close fellowship with him is to take away our peace when we sin against him and refuse to confess it (Ps. 32). Before he will restore our peace, he requires that

SCRIPTURE

Isaiah 26:3
He will keep in perfect peace all those who trust in him, whose thoughts turn often to the Lord!

John 14:27
I am leaving you with a gift— peace of mind and heart! And the peace I give isn't fragile like the peace the world gives. So don't be troubled or afraid.

Galatians 5:22
But when the Holy Spirit controls our lives he will produce this kind of fruit in us: love, joy, peace, patience, kindness, goodness, faithfulness, gentleness and self-control; and here there is no conflict with Jewish laws.

Philippians 4:6-9

Don't worry about anything; instead, pray about everything; tell God your needs and don't forget to thank him for his answers. If you do this you will experience God's peace, which is far more wonderful than the human mind can understand. His peace will keep your thoughts and your hearts quiet and at rest as you trust in Christ Jesus.

And now, brothers, as I close this letter let me say this one more thing: Fix your thoughts on what is true and good and right. Think about things that are pure and lovely, and dwell on the fine, good things in others. Think about all you can praise God for and be glad about.

we confess our sins to him. Then he will forgive and cleanse us from every sin (1 John 1:9).

Resist the devil. James writes that if we submit to God and resist the devil he will flee from us (James 4:7). One of those times we should resist the devil is when he points his finger at sins that we have already confessed. Another time is when he causes us to have feelings of guilt that are so general we cannot identify the sin which must be confessed. The devil hates God's people and wants to destroy our peace of mind, so he falsely accuses. In Revelation 12:10, the devil is called the Accuser. Don't ever let him get away with accusing you. Instead, resist him in the name of Jesus and he will have to flee from you.

Remember, when God the Holy Spirit convicts of sin, he puts his finger on something specific, a sin you have not confessed; and he does it because he loves you and wants you to enjoy his peace.

"So give yourself humbly to God. Resist the devil and he will flee from you" (James 4:7).

Praising and thanking the Lord is the most powerful way to resist the devil.

Forget the past. Although God has forgiven and cleansed us of our sins, we have a tendency to remember and impose self-condemnation. But the Apostle Paul tells us that he learned to forget his past sins and present imperfections, and look to Jesus Christ and his promises (Phil. 3:12-14). If Paul, who claimed to be the greatest of all sinners (1 Tim. 1:15), was able to forget his past, then we should also be able to accept God's forgiveness and forget. The one thing to remember is that God is able to forgive and forget our sins (Jer. 31:34). "He has removed our sins as far away from us as the east is from the west" (Ps. 103:12).

Micah the prophet wrote that because God has compassion on us, he "will tread our sins beneath [his] feet" and "will throw them into the depths of the ocean" (Mic. 7:19)! Someone has said that "God has thrown our sins into the depths of the ocean, and put up a No Fishing sign." We have no right bringing up those issues God has forgiven, buried, and forgotten. Forgetting what God has forgotten brings peace.

PRAYER

Pray that the one who is suffering from inner turmoil will take the necessary steps to find real peace in Christ. Encourage him to thank the Lord that in the midst of a troubled world, he can have the peace that Jesus gives, a peace which is far more wonderful than the human mind can understand (Phil. 4:7).

REFERENCES

Romans 5:1-9
We can have real peace because of what Christ has done for us

Romans 8:6
Following after the Holy Spirit leads to peace

Isaiah 32:16, 17
When God reigns as King there is peace

Isaiah 48:18
Obedience to God brings peace

SCRIPTURE

Acts 17:30, 31
God tolerated man's past ignorance about these things, but now he commands everyone to put away idols and worship only him. For he has set a day for justly judging the world by the man he has appointed; and has pointed him out by bringing him back to life again.

Luke 13:1-3
About this time he was informed that Pilate had butchered some Jews from Galilee as they were sacrificing at the Temple in Jerusalem. "Do you think they were worse sinners than other men from Galilee?" he asked. "Is that why they suffered? Not at all! And don't you realize that you also will perish unless you leave your evil ways and turn to God?"

PROBLEM

Repentance is turning away from sin and a self-centered life to a life lived under the lordship of Jesus Christ. This is a critically important—but often neglected—requirement for entering into or restoring a right relationship with God. Without genuine repentance we cannot live the Christian life.

BIBLICAL PERSPECTIVE

Repentance is the first step in beginning or restoring a right relationship with God (Acts 3:19). Repentance is also necessary when we have caused broken relationships with other persons (Luke 15:21).

COUNSEL

Man in his natural state is proud and self-centered. (See the section on PRIDE in the handbook.) The counselee may need to have a better understanding of this. The Scripture above will help provide the biblical perspective, as will the references below.

Find out if the counselee is ready to commit his life to Jesus as Lord. If so, lead him to salvation through repentance; he should ask God for forgiveness of his self-centeredness and his sins and should express a willingness to turn his back on the old life.

If there are specific sins that the counselee feels especially grieved about, you may want to refer to the sections of the handbook that deal with those—for example, VENGEANCE, OCCULT, SEXUAL SINS, BITTERNESS AND RESENTMENT, and others. Assure the counselee that no sin he has committed is too great to be forgiven by God.

PRAYER

A prayer like this may be appropriate if the counselee feels sincerely repentant: Father, I choose to turn from going my own way. I ask you to forgive and cleanse me from my rebellious way of life. I surrender completely to you. Come and be the Lord of my life. In Jesus' name, amen.

REFERENCES

Psalm 51
Example of true repentance—David

Exodus 9:27-35
Example of insincere repentance—Pharaoh

Romans 5:12-19
Sin is universal

1 John 3:4
Sin is against God

James 4:17
Knowledge and sin

Matthew 15:18-20
Defilement by evil thoughts and words

Romans 3:23
All have sinned

1 John 1:8, 9
God is faithful to forgive the repentant

READING
Repentance by Basilea Schlink

2 Corinthians 7:9, 10
Now I am glad I sent it, not because it hurt you, but because the pain turned you to God. It was a good kind of sorrow you felt, the kind of sorrow God wants his people to have, so that I need not come to you with harshness. For God sometimes uses sorrow in our lives to help us turn away from sin and seek eternal life. We should never regret his sending it. But the sorrow of the man who is not a Christian is not the sorrow of true repentance and does not prevent eternal death.

2 Peter 3:9
He isn't really being slow about his promised return, even though it sometimes seems that way. But he is waiting, for the good reason that he is not willing that any should perish, and he is giving more time for sinners to repent.

Luke 15:7
Well, in the same way heaven will be happier over one lost sinner who returns to God than over ninety-nine others who haven't strayed away!

SCRIPTURE

John 3:5
Jesus replied, "What I am telling you so earnestly is this: Unless one is born of water and the Spirit, he cannot enter the Kingdom of God."

Romans 3:23, 24
Yes, all have sinned; all fall short of God's glorious ideal; yet now God declares us "not guilty" of offending him if we trust in Jesus Christ, who in his kindness freely takes away our sins.

Romans 10:3
For they don't understand that Christ has died to make them right with God. Instead they are trying to make themselves good enough to gain God's favor by keeping the Jewish laws and customs, but that is not God's way of salvation.

1 John 1:9
But if we confess our sins to him, he can be depended on to forgive us and to cleanse us from every wrong. [And it is perfectly proper for God to do this for us because Christ died to wash away our sins.]

John 1:12
But to all who received him, he gave the right to become children of God. All they needed to do was to trust him to save them.

EXPLANATION

A Christian counselor's primary concern is always to find out whether a person has accepted Christ as his Savior. Almost all other problems he will encounter will have sin as their cause, which can only be dealt with by Christ. The Bible points the way to victory: salvation in Christ. Any other solutions to human needs and problems will be superficial and not treat the root cause of sin. Gaining forgiveness from God is the most important step a person can take.

BIBLICAL PERSPECTIVE

The Bible teaches that one must be born again in order to see the Kingdom of God, receive eternal life, find forgiveness of sins, and experience the indwelling of the Holy Spirit. Through faith one can become a child of God and a joint-heir with Christ. Salvation is to be received by faith in the death and resurrection of Christ for the atonement of sin. Repentance includes turning from sin and a self-centered life, and accepting the lordship of Jesus Christ. Salvation is totally a gift of God's grace. He chose us, called us, declared us "not guilty," filled us with Christ's goodness, and promised us his glory (Rom. 8:29, 30; Eph. 2:8, 9).

COUNSEL

If the counselee is not a Christian, explain to him his need. Share God's plan for salvation by grace through faith in Christ. Lead him to a decision, offering to pray with him. Refer him to a Christ-centered church fellowship that clearly teaches the Bible.

PRAYER

Ask the person to call on Jesus, to confess his
sins, and to receive him as Savior and Lord. If he
needs help to pray, ask him to follow you in a
prayer such as *Jesus, forgive me of my sin. I take
you at your Word that you forgive those who ask.
Be my Lord, as you are my Savior. I give myself to
you. I'm yours. Thank you for being faithful and
saving me. I've asked and I believe that you have
saved me. Amen.*

READING

"What Now?" tract from CBN
"It's All Yours!" tract from CBN

REFERENCES

Romans 6:23; Ephesians 2:8, 9; 2 Timothy 1:9
A gift

Matthew 3:1, 2; 10:32, 33; Luke 15:10; Acts
2:38, 39; 3:19; Romans 2:4; 10:9, 10; 2 Peter 3:9;
1 John 1:9
By repentance and confession

Mark 13:13; John 3:16; John 5:24; John 10:27, 28;
Romans 10:13; 1 Peter 1:3-5; 1 John 2:25; 5:13;
Revelation 3:20, 21
Assurance

SCRIPTURE

John 3:16
For God loved the world so much that he gave his only Son so that anyone who believes in him shall not perish, but have eternal life.

1 John 1:8, 9
If we say that we have no sin, we are only fooling ourselves, and refusing to accept the truth. But if we confess our sins to him, he can be depended on to forgive us and to cleanse us from every wrong. [And it is perfectly proper for God to do this for us because Christ died to wash away our sins.]

John 1:12
But to all who received him, he gave the right to become children of God. All they needed to do was to trust him to save them.

Revelation 3:20
Look! I have been standing at the door and I am constantly knocking. If anyone hears me calling him and opens the door, I will come in and fellowship with him and he with me.

PROBLEM
A child can use salvation counseling if he does not already know Jesus as Savior, or if, when asked whether he does, he is not certain.

BIBLICAL PERSPECTIVE
The Bible says that whoever calls on Jesus to save him will be saved (Rom. 10:13). Jesus came into the world to give us a new life that will never end (John 3:16). He is all-sufficient for our lives when we trust him.

COUNSEL
Use simplicity with a child. Do not confuse him with too many Scripture verses. Use illustrations from the Bible that meet him on his own age level.

First establish his need and desire to accept Jesus. Ask him if he wants to ask the Lord into his heart, according to the Bible's explanation of how to be saved. As you share a verse, have him repeat it after you. The Word will do its own work. Lead the child to pray in his own words and ask Jesus to forgive him of his sins and come into his heart. Then he should thank Jesus for answering his prayer. The child should be led into assurance of his salvation, through confirmation in the Word of God. The Holy Spirit also confirms this in his heart.

Explain the need for:

Obedience to God's Word
Immediate confession when he commits sin
Bible reading (if old enough to read)—memorizing
    verses
Talking to God in prayer
Christian friends
Telling others what happened to him and telling
    others about Jesus (e.g., family, Sunday school
    teacher, pastor, friends, etc.)
Attending church

PRAYER

After having lead the child in a simple prayer,
asking for forgiveness of sins and for Jesus to be
his Savior, pray again for the child and commit
him to the Lord.

READING

"Steps to Growing," tract from CBN. If the child
can write, have him write down chapters and
verses cited above.

FOR THE COUNSELOR:
Your Child, by Anna B. Mow
How to Raise Your Children for Christ by Andrew
    Murray
Teaching Your Child about God by Claudia Royal

FOR CHILDREN:
Arch Books, Christian Publications
Caterpillar Books, Christian Publications
Good News Bible, American Bible Society
The Living Bible, Tyndale House Publishers

HEALING

SCRIPTURE

Isaiah 53:4, 5
Yet it was our grief he bore, our sorrows that weighed him down. And we thought his troubles were a punishment from God, for his own sins! But he was wounded and bruised for our sins. He was beaten that we might have peace; he was lashed—and we were healed!

2 Corinthians 5:21
For God took the sinless Christ and poured into him our sins. Then, in exchange, he poured God's goodness into us!

1 John 5:14, 15
And we are sure of this, that he will listen to us whenever we ask him for anything in line with his will.

And if we really know he is listening when we talk to him and make our requests, then we can be sure that he will answer us.

Matthew 10:1
Jesus called his twelve disciples to him, and gave them authority to cast out evil spirits and to heal every kind of sickness and disease.

1 Corinthians 12:9
He gives special faith to another, and to someone else the power to heal the sick.

PROBLEM

Some physical, mental, or spiritual illness or infirmity is present. While most persons associate healing only with physical affliction, spirit, soul, and body are equally in need of wholeness, sometimes requiring more than prayer for healing. Professional treatment may be required.

BIBLICAL PERSPECTIVE

Both the Old and New Testaments speak of a God who is concerned for his children's welfare and who desires their health and wholeness. Christ came that we might have abundant life (John 10:10), and his earthly ministry included much healing. He indicated that the healings were a sign that the Kingdom of God was being instituted.

Diseases and infirmities are universal afflictions. Their presence is often unexplainable, though the Scriptures mention instances where illness is a punishment for sin (Deut. 28:61; Mic. 6:13; 1 Cor. 11:30). Often, as with Job, illness has no connection with sin. Whatever the cause, we know that God in his mercy desires our wholeness and desires that we act and pray to bring that wholeness about. We also know that marvelous works of healing still occur, in spite of the skepticism of many who reject the possibility of miracles.

COUNSEL

Steps to healing:

1. Believe and confess salvation (Rom. 10:10).
2. Agree in prayer with others (Matt. 18:19).
3. Take God at his word (Isa. 53:4, 5).
4. Receive healing by faith (James 5:14-16).
5. Continue in the Lord, learning and growing (Exod. 15:26).

After prayerfully listening to a counselee who desires healing, agree together in prayer that God is going to answer. Counsel and pray in faith, reminding the counselee to believe God's Word rather than trust in symptoms (James 1:6-8).

Keep in mind that there are barriers to healing, such as harboring iniquity in the heart (Ps. 66:18), involvement in cult or occult activity (Deut. 18:10-13), not having a wholehearted desire to be healed (that is, using the illness as a security blanket), doubt, worry, anxiety, bitterness, and others. These barriers need to be removed so the person can ask faithfully and confidently for God's power to act.

You cannot guarantee that a healing will occur, even if the counselee is a committed believer who has placed his confidence fully in God. You can provide assurance that God is merciful and just, and that all things—including both illness and health—work for good for those who love God. If a person is healed, God is glorified. If a person patiently endures affliction and continues to confess faith in God, that also brings glory to God. You will want to avoid the errors of either telling a person that healing will inevitably occur or of claiming that God is letting the person suffer for some reason (since you cannot know this for certain).

CAUTION: Do not under any circumstances advise the counselee to stop taking medicine or stop getting required medical attention. The counselee must make this decision for himself, and should do so only after consulting with his physician. It is not the task of the counselor to act as an expert in such matters.

In some instances God may use a Christian professional in his healing ministry such as a

James 5:14, 15
Is anyone sick? He should call for the elders of the church and they should pray over him and pour a little oil upon him, calling on the Lord to heal him. And their prayer, if offered in faith, will heal him, for the Lord will make him well; and if his sickness was caused by some sin, the Lord will forgive him.

pastor, counselor, physician, or psychologist (Matt. 9:12). It is extremely important to first seek the Lord through prayer for his guidance in all matters of healing.

PRAYER

Encourage the counselee to thank God for his providential care of his children. He should ask confidently for his blessing and express an earnest desire to be healed. The counselee should also express the need for strength to endure and guidance in the event that healing does not occur immediately.

REFERENCES

Romans 10:17
Faith

Deuteronomy 28:58-62
Warnings against disobedience

John 15:7
Abiding in Christ

John 11:1; Acts 9:36, 37; Philippians 2:25-27
Righteous people suffer

READING

Healing the Sick and Casting Out Demons by
    T. L. Osborn
Christian Healing Rediscovered by Roy Lawrence
Heal the Sick by Reginald East
Adventure in Adversity by Paul E. Billheimer

PROBLEM
The counselee may claim that something is wrong with his mind, or the counselor may discern a mental disorder or imbalance. The problem can often be determined by listening to the counselee and perceiving his need through the leading of the Holy Spirit.

BIBLICAL PERSPECTIVE
The Bible promises Christians a sound mind. However, mental illness may result from physiological damage, from demonic activity (Matt. 17:14-18), or from disobedience to God (Deut. 28:15, 28).

COUNSEL
Mental illness can be rooted in occult involvement, inordinate fear, demonic influences, willful disobedience to God, or physiological damage.

If the counselee speaks or acts strangely or perversely, suspect demonic activity or a rebellious attitude toward God. (See the section titled DELIVERANCE.)

Questions about what the counselee has been reading may indicate occult involvement. (See the section on the OCCULT.)

If you perceive evidence of suicidal tendencies, exaggerated fear, compulsiveness, or drug use, see sections of the handbook on those areas.

If the counselee is cooperative and rational, lead him through the steps to salvation, drawing on the power of the Holy Spirit.

Emphasize that the counselee himself is primarily responsible for maintaining his mental health. He cannot blame others for his mental state, and he alone is responsible to God for his behavior.

If the problem has a physiological cause (brain

SCRIPTURE
Isaiah 26:3
He will keep in perfect peace all those who trust in him, whose thoughts turn often to the Lord!

Philippians 4:8
And now, brothers, as I close this letter let me say this one more thing: Fix your thoughts on what is true and good and right. Think about things that are pure and lovely, and dwell on the fine, good things in others. Think about all you can praise God for and be glad about.

Luke 4:18, 19
The Spirit of the Lord is upon me; he has appointed me to preach Good News to the poor; he has sent me to heal the brokenhearted and to announce that captives shall be released and the blind shall see, that the downtrodden shall be freed from their oppressors, and that God is ready to give blessings to all who come to him.

Romans 12:2
Don't copy the behavior and customs of this world, but be a new and different person with a fresh newness in all you do and think. Then you will learn from your own experience how his ways will really satisfy you.

damage, for example), pray for healing and restoration of a sound, wholesome mind. Remind the counselee that, as a born-again believer, he may draw on the love and care of God. (See the section on HEALING.)

Encourage the counselee to participate in a church fellowship that is Christ-centered and clearly teaches the Bible, since he will need continuing love and counseling.

PRAYER

Pray for God's compassionate work in the person's life. Draw on God's promises that the oppressed will be set free. Seek the counselee's agreement with you that God is already answering this prayer.

REFERENCES

2 Timothy 1:7
Holy Spirit gives wisdom, strength, freedom from fear

Philippians 2:1-13; 4:8
God at work in us

Isaiah 26:3
Peace promised

Ephesians 5:15-21
Careful use of our time

Galatians 6:12-14
Carefulness in choosing teachers

Romans 12:2; Ephesians 4:23, 24
Being a renewed, transformed person

Galatians 3:13
Freedom from condemnation and bondage

Psalm 1:1-3
The delight of those who walk in God's ways

LIFE AND DEATH

SCRIPTURE

Deuteronomy 5:17
You must not murder.

Psalm 127:3
*Children are a gift from God;
they are his reward.*

Psalm 139:13-16
*You made all the delicate,
inner parts of my body, and
knit them together in my
mother's womb. Thank you
for making me so wonderfully
complex! It is amazing to
think about. Your workman-
ship is marvelous—and how
well I know it. You were there
while I was being formed in
utter seclusion! You saw me
before I was born and sched-
uled each day of my life before
I began to breathe. Every day
was recorded in your Book!*

_____

_____

_____

_____

_____

_____

_____

_____

_____

_____

_____

_____

PROBLEM

The counselor may encounter two problems:
(a) the woman who wants to have an abortion, or
(b) the woman who feels guilty because she has
had an abortion.

BIBLICAL PERSPECTIVE

It is wrong to take the life of an unborn child
because God commands, "You must not murder"
(Exod. 20:13). And the psalmist states that
"children are a gift from God; they are his reward"
(Ps. 127:3).

COUNSEL

(A) An expectant mother who is not married will
sometimes consider an abortion the only way to
deal with the shame of carrying an "illegitimate
child." Explain to her that in spite of her personal
sin, God is the one who is making those delicate
parts of her infant's body and knitting them
together inside her womb. God does not in any
way associate her sin with this new life which is
being created. She has no right to terminate
God's creative work.

(B) The woman who is suffering shame
because she has had an abortion needs to be
counseled and encouraged by a Christian. Yet,
often Christians shy away from such situations
because they fear that associating with sinners
will hurt their reputation; or they fear that by
harshly condemning her they will cause even
greater harm to the woman who has had the
abortion. Jesus sought opportunities to be with
sinners because he knew that without him
sinners were helpless. And he was harshly
criticized by the religious leaders of his day.

The counselor should inform the woman
who has had an abortion that she must now

repent. Assure her that God will forgive as promised in 1 John 1:9. Also warn her that any attempt at covering her sins instead of confessing will only compound the guilt, frustration, and broken relationships. Point her to the example of King David, who committed adultery with Bathsheba and tried to cover up his sin by having Bathsheba's husband killed in battle (2 Sam. 11).

Once the woman has repented, give assurance of salvation and show her in God's Word how the Holy Spirit can help her to live a holy, joyful, and effective Christian life. Finally, encourage her to talk with her minister, or refer her to a pastor who believes and teaches God's Word. Also try to get her into an unwed mothers' group, but do not give medical advice. Only doctors have that right.

PRAYER
Pray that God will give her the strength and courage to face all that is ahead. Praise and thank God that he has not punished us as we deserve for all our sins. Thank him for accepting and forgiving her, and for giving her the ability to forgive herself.

FOLLOW-UP
Read the story of King David in 2 Samuel 2 and 12.

REFERENCES

Psalm 127:3
For pre-abortion counselee

Psalm 139:13-16
God knows a person from conception

Proverbs 31
Ideal woman and mother

Matthew 6:33
Give God first place in your life

Philippians 3:13, 14
Forget the past

Isaiah 40:31; Philippians 4:13
God will renew your strength

_____

_____

_____

_____

_____

_____

_____

_____

_____

SCRIPTURE

Job 5:15
God saves the fatherless and the poor from the grasp of these oppressors.

Psalm 34:1, 7
I will praise the Lord no matter what happens. I will constantly speak of his glories and grace.

For the Angel of the Lord guards and rescues all who reverence him.

Psalm 91:1, 11, 12, 15, 16
We live within the shadow of the Almighty, sheltered by the God who is above all gods.

For he orders his angels to protect you wherever you go. They will steady you with their hands to keep you from stumbling against the rocks on the trail.

"When he calls on me I will answer; I will be with him in trouble, and rescue him and honor him. I will satisfy him with a full life and give him my salvation."

John 10:10
The thief's purpose is to steal, kill and destroy. My purpose is to give life in all its fullness.

PROBLEM

The desire or decision to kill oneself is in most cases the result of a state of acute depression. It may be brought on by health problems, pain, or the inability to handle frustration. Irresponsible behavior may produce the strong desire to destroy oneself or to leave the world. Demon influences may be involved, as may cultic teaching that results in brainwashed behavior.

BIBLICAL PERSPECTIVE

Our hope is in God and our strength is in him (Ps. 42:11). There are times when God seems far away and our prayers go unanswered, but the Bible teaches that God brings deliverance, healing, and eternal hope. Despair seems to be inevitable in every human life, but it need not persist, for we are assured that God loves us and gives our life meaning and purpose.

COUNSEL

NOTE: If the counselee appears truly suicidal or has already taken steps (swallowing poison, for example), obtain the following information in a calm manner so as not to further alarm the person: name, phone number, address, next of kin (and their phone number). Have another person report this information to the police or rescue team while you keep the person talking. If possible get someone to pray for you and the counselee while you are counseling.

The first step in counseling the suicide case is finding out what has driven him to such a drastic step. Find out what the underlying problems are. Ask the person what is bothering him and accept the answers as totally sincere until you learn otherwise. Do not play down the importance of the person's perceived problems. Listen carefully and with compassion. Offer godly counsel as the Holy Spirit gives you guidance in your responses to the counselee.

Refer the person (if they are, at this point, only considering suicide and have not yet made the attempt) to a strong and caring pastor of a Christ-centered church fellowship. Notify the pastor that you have talked with the counselee.

The counselor's main function may be to emphasize hope, which is joyful expectation rooted in God's promises (Rom. 15:4).

PRAYER

Pray that God will send ministering angels to the person (Heb. 1:14). Ask God to show his love to the person. Be sensitive to the Spirit's leading in how to pray further.

_____

_____

_____

_____

_____

_____

_____

_____

REFERENCES

Psalms 40; 42; 43
Hope

Psalm 51
Prayer for God's mercy

Psalm 73
Confession of faith in God's mercy and power to deliver

Romans 8:1-14; Isaiah 1:18
Assurance of God's grace

Ephesians 2:8, 9
Saved by God's grace

Galatians 5:22, 23
Fruit of the Spirit

Philippians 4:6-8
God's peace which passes all understanding

Philippians 4:19
God's supply for all our needs

Hebrews 7:25
Jesus as Savior of all who come to him

Matthew 7:7-11
Ask, seek, and knock to receive from God

Matthew 6:25-34
God gives us what we need

PRAYER

SCRIPTURE

Deuteronomy 9:9, 15-18
(The extended absolute fast)
I was on the mountain at the time, receiving the contract which Jehovah had made with you—the stone tablets with the laws inscribed upon them. I was there for forty days and forty nights, and all that time I ate nothing. I didn't even take a drink of water.

I came down from the burning mountain, holding in my hands the two tablets inscribed with the laws of God. There below me I could see the calf you had made in your terrible sin against the Lord your God. How quickly you turned away from him! I lifted the tablets high above my head and dashed them to the ground! I smashed them before your eyes! Then, for another forty days and nights I lay before the Lord, neither eating bread nor drinking water, for you had done what the Lord hated most, thus provoking him to great anger.

Luke 4:1, 2 (The extended partial or absolute fast)
Then Jesus, full of the Holy Spirit, left the Jordan River, being urged by the Spirit out into the barren wastelands of Judea, where Satan tempted him for forty days. He ate nothing all that time, and was very hungry.

DESCRIPTION

Fasting, like so many other things in Scripture, is a physical symbol of a spiritual reality. The withholding of food from the body is of no spiritual value unless it is done deliberately when we desire nothing but to seek God.

Types of fast:

Absolute fast: no food or drink
Normal fast: limited time
Partial fast: limited diet

BIBLICAL PERSPECTIVE

"I have esteemed the words of his mouth more than my necessary food" (Job 23:12).

COUNSEL

The Bible clearly states that one should fast, but a problem arises when we ask the question, "Why?" One's motivation is extremely important (1 Cor. 4:5).

Jesus tells us that the hypocrites fast to show other people that they are fasting (Matt. 6:16). As Christians we are called to fast for spiritual purposes in secret (Matt. 6:18).

Fasting is a response to God—he speaks; we stop and give him our attention. Unless we are responding from the heart to a word from God, our fasting may be motivated by self-interest.

The motives for fasting are spoken of in Isaiah 58:6, 7. The results of a chosen fast of God are shown in Isaiah 58:8. Principally the motives acceptable to God are those where one's desire is to seek the Lord and intercede for a person or situation. The results are personally edifying as well as beneficial to whom or whatever the fast was for.

PRAYER

Pray with the individual, asking God to help him be sensitive to the Holy Spirit as God seeks to draw him closer and to purify and bless him.

REFERENCES

Isaiah 58
Motive and reward of fasting

Acts 13:2, 3, 14-23
Fasting and God's commission to serve

Joel 1:14, 2:12
Fasting enjoined

Matthew 6:17-21
Fast privately

READING

The Adventures of Fasting by James Beall
God's Chosen Fast by Arthur Wallis

Acts 9:8, 9 (The normal fast)
As Paul picked himself up off the ground, he found that he was blind. He had to be led into Damascus and was there three days, blind, going without food and water all that time.

Daniel 10:2-3 NIV (The partial fast)
At that time I, Daniel, mourned for three weeks. I ate no choice food; no meat or wine touched my lips . . .

_____

_____

_____

_____

SCRIPTURE

Romans 8:26, 27, 34
And in the same way—by our faith—the Holy Spirit helps us with our daily problems and in our praying. For we don't even know what we should, pray for, nor how to pray as we should; but the Holy Spirit prays for us with such feeling that it cannot be expressed in words. And the Father who knows all hearts knows, of course, what the Spirit is saying as he pleads for us in harmony with God's own will.

Who then will condemn us? Will Christ? No! For he is the one who died for us and came back to life again for us and is sitting at the place of highest honor next to God, pleading for us there in heaven.

1 Timothy 2:1
Here are my directions: Pray much for others, plead for God's mercy upon them; give thanks for all he is going to do for them.

Hebrews 7:25
He is able to save completely all who come to God through him. Since he will live forever, he will always be there to remind God that he has paid for their sins with his blood.

DESCRIPTION

To intercede in prayer and in the authority of Jesus is one of the greatest privileges a Christian can have. It is part of our ministry; it is one way we can express our deep concern for their well being. Intercession is the constructive answer to our involvement in others' lives.

BIBLICAL PERSPECTIVE

In the face of all adversity, sin, illness, satanic attack—God's word to his people is to intercede (Isa. 59:16).

COUNSEL

The two main aspects of intercession are: (1) to intercede with God, and (2) to stand with the other person against evil. Ezekiel points out that an intercessor must be willing to feel and bear the burden of those for whom he intercedes (Gal. 6:2).

These ten principles of intercession are tried and proven effective (from Joy Dawson's "Some Principles for Effective Intercession"):

1. Praise God for the privilege of engaging in the same wonderful ministry as the Lord Jesus (Heb. 7:25). Praise God for the privilege of cooperating with him in the affairs of men.

2. Make very sure your heart is clean before God by giving the Holy Spirit time to convict, in case you have any unconfessed sin (Pss. 66:18; 139:23, 24). Check carefully to see if you bear any resentment toward anyone (Matt. 6:12; Mark 11:25). Job had to forgive his friends for their wrong judging of him before he could pray effectively for them (Job 42:10).

3. Acknowledge that you can't really pray without the direction and energy of the Holy Spirit (Rom. 8:26). Ask God to utterly control you by his Spirit, receive by faith that he does, and thank him (Eph. 5:18; Heb. 11:6).
4. Die to your own imaginations, desires, and burdens (Prov. 3:5, 6; 28:26; Isa. 55:8).
5. Deal aggressively with the enemy. Denounce him in the all-powerful name of Jesus Christ, and with the sword of the Spirit—the Word of God (James 4:7).
6. Praise God now in faith for the prayer time you are going to have. He is a remarkable God and will do that which is consistent with his character.
7. Wait before God in silent expectancy, listening for his direction (Ps. 62:5; Micah 7:7; Ps. 81:11-13).
8. In obedience and faith, utter what God brings to your mind (John 10:27). Keep asking God for direction in relation to who or what you are praying, expecting him to give it to you. He will (Ps. 32:8). Make sure you don't move on to the next subject until you've given God time to discharge all he wants to say to you regarding this particular burden, especially when you're praying in a group. Be encouraged by the lives of Moses, Daniel, Paul, and Anna, that God gives revelation to those who make intercession a way of life.
9. Always have your Bible with you in order to receive confirmation or direction (Ps. 119:105).
10. When God ceases to bring things to your mind for which to pray, praise him for what he is doing. Remind yourself that everything is for God's glory (Rom. 11:36).

Isaiah 59:16
He saw no one was helping you, and wondered that no one intervened. Therefore he himself stepped in to save you through his mighty power and justice.

A warning: God knows the weakness of the human heart toward pride, and if we speak of what God has revealed and done in intercession, it may lead to committing this sin. God shares his secrets with those who are able to keep them. There may come a time when he definitely prompts us to share, but unless this happens, we should remain silent (Luke 2:19; 9:36).

PRAYER

Ask God to reveal those needs for which intercession should be made. Thank and praise him for calling intercessors and equipping them with gifts for lifting burdens and delivering the saints and the needy.

FOLLOW-UP

List those who need your intercession. Record dates for the beginning of the intercession and the answers.

Keep a log (diary) of Scripture, circumstances, words of knowledge or wisdom, impressions, and thoughts that come to you. Search these for a pattern in which God is speaking to you.

READING

With Christ in the School of Prayer by Andrew Murray

PROBLEM

There are times when we have difficulty offering praise to the Lord. This comes from being too involved in our personal circumstances, which leads us to take our eyes off of the Lord. This brings about discouragement and leaves little or no desire to praise the Lord.

BIBLICAL PERSPECTIVE

When honor and respect are given, honor and respect will be received. The person who honors God will be honored by God (1 Sam. 2:30). A significant part of the Christian life is the adoration and praise of God (Heb. 13:15).

COUNSEL

Praising God is ministering to God. The Old Testament priests ministered to God by offering sacrifices of animals or food, and Christians now minister to God by offering sacrifices of praise (Heb. 13:15). A sacrifice of praise is given when a person continues to praise God even in the face of doubts, adversity, temptation, and lack of desire to praise. The counselee may need to be reminded that God is pleased when we offer praise under such circumstances, and that he is glorified when his people offer praise and thanksgiving during the bad times. The Christian should offer sacrifices of praise until (and after) joy and victory come. We should praise God continually in the Spirit so that the Spirit may not be quenched (1 Thess. 5:19).

PRAYER

Give thanks to God and praise him with the counselee. As you praise God, expect him to minister to both you and the counselee.

SCRIPTURE

1 Thessalonians 5:18
No matter what happens, always be thankful, for this is God's will for you who belong to Christ Jesus.

Ephesians 1:3
How we praise God, the Father of our Lord Jesus Christ, who has blessed us with every blessing in heaven because we belong to Christ.

Hebrews 13:15
With Jesus' help we will continually offer our sacrifice of praise to God by telling others of the glory of his name.

Deuteronomy 10:21
He is your praise and he is your God, the one who has done mighty miracles you yourselves have seen.

Psalm 149:5
Let his people rejoice in this honor. Let them sing for joy as they lie upon their beds.

REFERENCES

Patterns of praise:

Psalms 33:2; 57:8; 150:3-5
Praise with music

Revelation 19:1-7; Ephesians 5:19; Psalms 40:3; 71:8
Praise with the mouth

Psalm 47:1; 63:4; 134:2
Praise with the hands

2 Samuel 6:14; Psalm 149:3
Praise with dancing

Results of praise:

Psalm 149:1-4
Praise delights God

Psalm 50:23
Praise glorifies God

Jude 20
Praise edifies the faithful

READING
Prison to Praise by Merlin Carothers
Power in Praise by Merlin Carothers
Praise Works by Merlin Carothers
Pocket Praise by Robert C. Savage

DESCRIPTION

Prayer is communication with God, petitioning him for needs, asking for his healing for problems, and offering him thanksgiving and praise.

BIBLICAL PERSPECTIVE

A Christian addresses the Father directly when he prays, through the authority which Jesus Christ designated to Christians (John 14:12-14; Matt. 6:6). A non-Christian needs first to call upon Jesus to save him before he can pray to the Father (Rom. 10:13).

COUNSEL

Authentic prayer is possible when one is "closeted" with the Father, shutting out all else, keeping one's mind on him (Matt. 6:6). Such prayer demands honor, respect, and recognition of God's nature and authority.

God already knows our needs and has the answers for us, even before we call upon him (Isa. 65:24). Therefore we can praise him ahead of time for what he will do in our lives. If we do not know how to pray for a particular need, we can pray for discernment through the Spirit. He will teach us how to pray, bring needs to our hearts, and lift burdens as they are met.

The Christian is to pray without ceasing: "Always keep on praying. No matter what happens, always be thankful" (1 Thess. 5:17, 18). This is the key to communion with God through one's lifetime.

PRAYER

In simplicity, offer a prayer for the counselee. Then ask the counselee to offer a prayer of thanksgiving to God for answering prayer.

SCRIPTURE

1 Peter 5:6
If you will humble yourselves under the mighty hand of God, in his good time he will lift you up.

Ephesians 3:12
Now we can come fearlessly right into God's presence, assured of his glad welcome when we come with Christ and trust in him.

Psalm 95:2
Come before him with thankful hearts. Let us sing him psalms of praise.

Matthew 26:39
He went forward a little, and fell face downward on the ground, and prayed, "My Father! If it is possible, let this cup be taken away from me. But I want your will, not mine."

REFERENCES

John 14:12-14
In Jesus' name

2 Timothy 1:3
Pure conscience

Isaiah 56:7
Joyfully

1 Thessalonians 5:17; Luke 18:1
Continually

Psalm 66:18
Penitentially

1 John 5:14, 15; Matthew 21:22
Believing

Romans 8:28; 1 Thessalonians 5:18
In all circumstances

Ephesians 6:18
For all Christians everywhere

1 Timothy 2:8
Everywhere

FOLLOW-UP

Study "prayer" with a concordance and your Bible.

READING

Favor: the Road to Success by Bob Buess
"Answered Prayer," tract from CBN
Lectures on Revivals of Religion, chapter 4, by
    Charles Finney

GOD'S PRINCIPLES

SCRIPTURE

Acts 2:1
Seven weeks had gone by since Jesus' death and resurrection, and the Day of Pentecost had now arrived. As the believers met together that day. (Great spiritual blessing followed because the believers met together.)

Acts 4:24, 31
Then all the believers united in this prayer. . . . After this prayer, the building where they were meeting shook and they were all filled with the Holy Spirit and boldly preached God's message.

Acts 12:5 (When Peter was in prison for preaching the gospel)
Earnest prayer was going up to God from the church for his safety all the time he was in prison. (The rest of the chapter tells how God answered the prayer of the believers and freed Peter from prison.)

DESCRIPTION

The principle of agreement is basic to the Kingdom of God. When we, by faith and repentance, enter into an agreement, or "covenant," with God, making Christ the Lord of our life, we become children of God and heirs of eternal life. All of this is possible because Jesus made atonement for our sins by shedding his blood. The word *atonement* means "at-one-ment." At the same time, we enter into an agreement or "covenant" with other Christians, because we are now brothers and sisters in God's family. The principle, then, is that because we stand in such a favored position with God and his earthly children, we possess great spiritual power.

BIBLICAL PERSPECTIVE

Our unbelief gives birth to disagreement and disobedience. But belief in God sows the seed of agreement, which results in obedience. This is what Jesus meant when he said, "Yes, I am the Vine; you are the branches. Whoever lives in me and I in him shall produce a large crop of fruit. For apart from me you can't do a thing. . . . If you stay in me and obey my commands, you may ask any request you like, and it will be granted!" (John 15:5, 7). Agreement with fellow believers is also necessary for spiritual power. Jesus said, "If two of you agree down here on earth concerning anything you ask for, my Father in heaven will do it for you" (Matt. 18:19).

COUNSEL

Obedience to Scripture demonstrates agreement with God. When we take the time and make the necessary effort to agree in prayer with another believer, we please God and can expect him to answer as he has promised. Live obediently. Agree in prayer with other believers.

When you pray, be certain in your own mind that you believe God and agree with what he wants. James puts it this way: "But when you ask him, be sure that you really expect him to tell you, for a doubtful mind will be as unsettled as a wave of the sea that is driven and tossed by the wind. . . . If you don't ask with faith, don't expect the Lord to give you any solid answer" (James 1:6-8).

You can experience great spiritual power and confidence when you learn to live in agreement with God and your fellow believers. Your walk with God can be a delight; your family life will be richer.

PRAYER

Emphasize the need for belief and obedience to God and agreement with fellow believers. Expect God to change attitudes and relationships.

REFERENCES

Amos 3:3
Israel's disobedience hindered her walk with God

2 Kings 5:13, 14
Naaman was healed when he obeyed

2 Samuel 12:13
David agreed with God and was forgiven

Jonah 3:3-5
When Jonah agreed and obeyed, God went to work

SCRIPTURE

Psalm 86:15
*But you are merciful and
gentle, Lord, slow in getting
angry, full of constant loving-
kindness and of truth.*

Psalm 27:14
*Don't be impatient. Wait for
the Lord, and he will come
and save you! Be brave,
stouthearted, and coura-
geous. Yes, wait and he will
help you.*

Proverbs 8:17-19
*I love all who love me. Those
who search for me shall surely
find me. Unending riches,
honor, justice and righteousness are mine to distribute.
My gifts are better than the
purest gold or sterling silver!*

John 12:26
*If these Greeks want to be my
disciples, tell them to come
and follow me, for my servants must be where I am.
And if they follow me, the
Father will honor them.*

Genesis 39:21
*But the Lord was with Joseph
there, too, and was kind to
him by granting him favor
with the chief jailer.*

Matthew 17:20
*"Because of your little faith,"
Jesus told them. "For if you
had faith even as small as a
tiny mustard seed you could
say to this mountain, 'Move!'
and it would go far away.
Nothing would be impos-
sible."*

DESCRIPTION

One of the principles of the Kingdom of God is
that God favors a just man (Prov. 12:2). For the
righteous, favor with God is assured. Victory is
promised over bad experiences, fear, and
negativism. Though we have needs and pressures, we have God's promise of resolution.

BIBLICAL PERSPECTIVE

Jesus came that we might have a full, meaningful
life (John 10:10). While God's people do suffer
misfortunes, it is God's will that they live an
abundant life, thus bringing glory to his name.

COUNSEL

As children of God, we can ask for God's grace
to be upon us and remember the promises that
we will flourish and prosper (Prov. 14:11; Pss.
84:11; 92:12). But to remain within God's will
requires that we not harbor iniquity in our
hearts, for he will not hear the prayers of those
who do not confess sin (Ps. 66:17-20).

Favor from God comes because of his love and
grace, not because of anything we do. God does
not bless out of obligation but out of love. We
should not use God's favor toward us as a reason
for pride; rather, it is a reason to praise the
sovereign God for his kindness.

The counselee may be despairing over some
defeat in life. Remind him that life itself is a gift
from God and cause for praise. Ask the counselee
to name instances where God has blessed him.

PRAYER

Praise and thank God for his favor upon the
counselee.

READING

Pocket Promise Book by David Wilkerson
Pocket Praise by Robert C. Savage

PROBLEM

Few Christians ever progress in their life in Christ to any degree of spiritual maturity. But when Jesus said, "The thief's purpose is to steal, kill, and destroy. My purpose is to give life in all its fullness" (John 10:10), he was expressing God's desire that we should become all that we can be in Christ Jesus.

BIBLICAL PERSPECTIVE

The counselee can have an overcoming, victorious life because of the shed blood of Jesus and because of what he can become in Christ (Rev. 12:10, 11).

The Bible says that as one thinks in his heart, so has one become (Luke 6:45). The counselee will think in a godly way as he receives the full counsel of God. As he grows in spiritual knowledge and experience, he will gain spiritual maturity and the abundant life that God promised.

COUNSEL

Advise and assist the counselee through the following steps:

1. Becoming born again. Death reigns over us from our birth (Rom. 5:12) because of our sinful nature of pride versus submission to God. (1 John 2:16). We think and behave after the lusts (appetites) of our flesh and our eyes, and after the dictates of the pride of life (Gal. 5:19-21).

Show the counselee that Jesus came to change his relationship with God (John 3:16). Encourage him to pray, to confess and repent of his sins. Tell him that God will give him power (authority) to become a son of God (Rom. 10:13; 1 John 1:9; John 1:12).

2. Being baptized in the Holy Spirit. After the counselee has been saved (or "born again,"

SCRIPTURE

Romans 10:13
Anyone who calls upon the name of the Lord will be saved.

Acts 1:8
But when the Holy Spirit has come upon you, you will receive power to testify about me with great effect, to the people in Jerusalem, throughout Judea, in Samaria, and to the ends of the earth, about my death and resurrection.

Luke 11:13
And if even sinful persons like yourselves give children what they need, don't you realize that your heavenly Father will do at least as much, and give the Holy Spirit to those who ask for him?

Ephesians 4:11, 12
Some of us have been given special ability as apostles; to others he has given the gift of being able to preach well; some have special ability in winning people to Christ, helping them to trust him as their Savior; still others have a gift for caring for God's people as a shepherd does his sheep, leading and teaching them in the ways of God. Why is it that he gives us these special abilities to do certain things best? It is that God's people will be equipped to do better work for him, building up the Church, the body of Christ, to a position of strength and maturity.

Ephesians 6:11
Put on all of God's armor so that you will be able to stand safe against all strategies and tricks of Satan.

Galatians 5:22, 23
But when the Holy Spirit controls our lives he will produce this kind of fruit in us: love, joy, peace, patience, kindness, goodness, faithfulness, gentleness and self-control; and here there is no conflict with Jewish laws.

1 Corinthians 12:7-10
The Holy Spirit displays God's power through each of us as a means of helping the entire church. To one person the Spirit gives the ability to give wise advice; someone else may be especially good at studying and teaching, and this is his gift from the same Spirit. He gives special faith to another, and to someone else the power to heal the sick. He gives power for doing miracles to some, and to others power to prophesy and preach. He gives someone else the power to know whether evil spirits are speaking through those who claim to be giving God's messages— or whether it is really the Spirit of God who is speaking. Still another person is able to speak in languages he never learned; and others, who do not know the language either, are given power to understand what he is saying.

"adopted," "redeemed," "converted"—all terms describing the experience of salvation) he will find he needs power to live the Christian life. This power is available when one is baptized with the Holy Spirit. The Holy Spirit will comfort, guide, help, and empower the counselee (Luke 11:13; Joel 2:28-32; John 14 and 16; Acts 1:8; Mark 16:16-20). Through the Holy Spirit, his experiences will be similar to those of the first disciples.

He can pray alone and receive the baptism with the Holy Spirit (Luke 11:13), or a Christ-centered friend or pastor can pray with him and help him in his understanding of the Holy Spirit.

3. The fruit of the Spirit. As the Holy Spirit edifies the counselee's spirit, he can begin replacing his worldly, fleshly nature with God's nature (Gal. 5:22, 23). Receiving the character traits of God is perhaps the most important need a Christian has. The Holy Spirit will work in every experience and detail of one's life to produce the fullness of the nature of God (the fruit of the Spirit).

4. Ministries of the Spirit. God has set in the Church five gifted ministries: apostles (missionaries who are sent to preach the gospel and establish churches); prophets (who proclaim God's written or newly revealed, prophetic word to the church); evangelists (who proclaim his righteousness, holiness, mercy, love, etc., and who call people to turn from sinfulness to repentance); and pastors and teachers (providing spiritual aid and nurture). For one to be spiritually built up in the Lord (Eph. 4:11-13), it is important to attend a church fellowship regularly where these ministries are present.

5. God's armor. God's armor is: truth, righteousness, the gospel of peace, faith, salvation, and God's Word (the sword or weapon). It is received, put on, and put to use as a result of knowing God's Word. Then, like a soldier, the Christian must maintain his equipment (spiritual armor and arms) through Bible study, the ministry of the church, and diligent prayer (Eph. 6:11-18). With God's armor, the counselee will be able to stand against spiritual wickedness in all its forms, whether in the physical or spiritual realm.

6. Gifts of the Spirit. Every Christian has a spiritual gift (not necessarily supernatural) of some kind, depending on his faith (1 Pet. 4:10; Rom. 12:3-9, "motivational gifts"). The baptism with the Holy Spirit makes the counselee eligible for the supernatural gifts of the Spirit to be manifested through him as he carries out the works of Christ (John 14:12). This includes overcoming sin, sickness, and evil, and ministering to others (2 Cor. 10:4, 5). Every Spirit-filled Christian can minister through the supernatural gifts (1 Cor. 12:7-10, 27-31).

7. Kingdom principles. In practicing the principles of God's Kingdom, one can receive the fulfillment of God's promises. One or more of the following principles will apply to most or all problems that are encountered. Advise the counselee to become thoroughly familiar with the following kingdom principles; encourage him to practice them for victory and growth in his life.

1. Praise to God. He honors those who honor him (1 Sam. 2:30). The counselee needs to honor God, the Problem Solver, rather than honoring a problem, sin, temptation, illness, etc.
2. Submission to God (his Word). The place of obedience is the place of power (Matt. 18:19). Disobedience brings only defeat.
3. Reciprocity. As he gives, it will be given in

return, in even greater measure (Luke 6:38). As he does for others and for God, it will be done for him.

4. Favor. God favors a just man. He honors those who serve him (John 12:26). The counselee must learn to serve God and walk in his favor.

5. Fasting. He should desire to hear from God more than he desires food to eat (Job 23:12). If he fasts on behalf of another, or for his own need, God's reward to him will include healing, personal recognition, protection, favor, and his sure guidance (Isa. 58:6-12).

6. Intercession. To intercede means to stand up for those in need, as a friend or defender (Isa. 59:16). God acts in response to the prayers of a Christian.

In summary, show the counselee that he should be satisfied with nothing less than God's full counsel for him. As a maturing, equipped Christian, he will be an overcomer in the world and able to teach others as well.

PRAYER

Encourage the counselee to thank and praise God daily as he learns, meditates, and grows in the basic areas of God's full counsel. Advise him to pray for others he knows who need God's fullness in their lives.

FOLLOW-UP

Daily read the Psalms and Proverbs for worship experiences and wisdom.

PROBLEM
The counselee is seeking God's will regarding a particular aspect of life; he needs God's leading for a specific decision.

BIBLICAL PERSPECTIVE
God has a plan for us in all matters. If we seek him first before making our plans, rather than leaning upon our own understanding, he will meet all of our needs and direct our path. (Prov. 3:5-6).

COUNSEL
There are three areas in which God's will can be revealed: his Word, the Spirit's leading, and peace within one's circumstances. When all three of these areas are in agreement in a person's life, it is a good sign of God's leading and his will.

PRAYER
Thank and praise God for revealing his will to the counselee. As you do so, expect other verification: a word from God, circumstances bringing to pass what was revealed, and the Scriptures providing a confirming message.

REFERENCES
Psalm 73:24
God's counsel

Isaiah 42:16
Guidance along unknown paths

Proverbs 16:1
Our lives are in God's hands

Proverbs 21:1
God turns hearts of men

Proverbs 21:2
He knows our motives

READING
Obtaining God's Guidance by Ralph Mahoney

SCRIPTURE
Matthew 6:33
And he will give them to you if you give him first place in your life and live as he wants you to.

Proverbs 3:4-6
If you want favor with both God and man, and a reputation for good judgment and common sense, then trust the Lord completely; don't ever trust yourself. In everything you do, put God first, and he will direct you and crown your efforts with success.

Psalm 25:9
He will teach the ways that are right and best to those who humbly turn to him.

John 16:13
When the Holy Spirit, who is truth, comes, he shall guide you into all truth, for he will not be presenting his own ideas, but will be passing on to you what he has heard. He will tell you about the future.

James 3:17
But the wisdom that comes from heaven is first of all pure and full of quiet gentleness.

SCRIPTURE

2 Corinthians 5:18, 19
All these new things are from God who brought us back to himself through what Christ Jesus did. And God has given us the privilege of urging everyone to come into his favor and be reconciled to him. For God was in Christ, restoring the world to himself, no longer counting men's sins against them but blotting them out. This is the wonderful message he has given us to tell others.

Colossians 1:20
It was through what his Son did that God cleared a path for everything to come to him—all things in heaven and on earth—for Christ's death on the cross has made peace with God for all by his blood.

Matthew 5:23, 24
So if you are standing before the altar in the Temple, offering a sacrifice to God, and suddenly remember that a friend has something against you, leave your sacrifice there beside the altar and go and apologize and be reconciled to him, and then come and offer your sacrifice to God.

PROBLEM

Broken relationships intensify other problems and lead to emotional and even physical illness. Bitterness, anger, and frustration that follow in the wake of broken relationships can hinder the possibility of healing the relationships. Reconciliation is healing, the bringing of peace between parents and children, husbands and wives, labor and management, friend and friend, God and man.

BIBLICAL PERSPECTIVE

The great theme of the New Testament is that God is, in Christ, reconciling the world to himself (2 Cor. 5:19). God wants us to be reconciled to him and wants all broken relationships to be healed.

COUNSEL

The need for reconciliation is primarily the need to come to agreement, first with God and then with other persons. The counselee will probably want to talk about what to do to make agreement come about. The fact that he expresses concern about the broken relationship indicates that he already desires healing.

Determine whether the person has been born again. If he has not, salvation through repentance is a prime need. (See the section on REPENTANCE in the handbook.) Emphasize the necessity of repentance before a right relationship with God can begin. Stress God's forgiving nature and the role of Christ in bridging the gap between us and God.

If reconciliation of relationships with other persons is needed, refer to the Scripture passages above (especially the passages from Matthew). Emphasize the necessity of being at peace with other people if we are to be in a right relationship with God.

Where reconciliation of spouses or parents and children is needed, see the sections on DIVORCE, PARENT-CHILD RELATIONSHIPS, FORGIVENESS, ENVY/JEALOUSY, and MARITAL RELATIONS.

Remind the counselee that as Christians we are obligated to take steps toward healing broken relationships. Remind him that we are also to pray for the salvation of others so that they might be reconciled to God and begin to heal broken relationships in their own lives.

PRAYER

Encourage the counselee to seek the Lord's guidance as he tries to discern any hindrances (bitterness, resentment, fear of failure) to reconciliation in his life. Pray that he will see the necessity for reconciliation and will take steps toward it.

REFERENCES

Romans 12
Doing good

Luke 17:4
Continuing forgiveness of others

Ephesians 4:31, 32
Forgiving because God forgives

READING
Prison to Praise by Merlin Carothers
Anger: Defusing the Bomb by Ray Burwick
The Freedom of Forgiveness by David Augsburger

Matthew 5:25, 26
Come to terms quickly with your enemy before it is too late and he drags you into court and you are thrown into a debtor's cell, for you will stay there until you have paid the last penny.

Matthew 18:15-17
If a brother sins against you, go to him privately and confront him with his fault. If he listens and confesses it, you have won back a brother. But if not, then take one or two others with you and go back to him again, proving everything you say by these witnesses. If he still refuses to listen, then take your case to the church, and if the church's verdict favors you, but he won't accept it, then the church should excommunicate him.

REBELLION

SCRIPTURE

Revelation 2:4, 5
Yet there is one thing wrong; you don't love me as at first! Think about those times of your first love (how different now!) and turn back to me again and work as you did before; or else I will come and remove your candlestick from its place among the churches.

Psalm 51:1-12
O loving and kind God, have mercy. Have pity upon me and take away the awful stain of my transgressions. Oh, wash me, cleanse me from this guilt. Let me be pure again. For I admit my shameful deed—it haunts me day and night. . . . Sprinkle me with the cleansing blood and I shall be clean again. Wash me and I shall be whiter than snow. . . . Don't keep looking at my sins—erase them from your sight. Create in me a new, clean heart, O God, filled with clean thoughts and right desires. . . . Restore to me again the joy of your salvation, and make me willing to obey you.

Hosea 14:4
Then I will cure you of idolatry and faithlessness, and my love will know no bounds, for my anger will be forever gone!

PROBLEM

Backsliding is losing interest in God (1 Kings 11:9, 10) and not loving Christ "as at first" (Rev. 2:4). Backsliding is first a condition of the heart— a cold or rebellious heart and sinful attitudes— then it becomes evident in one's life-style.

BIBLICAL PERSPECTIVE

Backsliding can be prevented. A believer is in danger of backsliding unless he takes such scriptural precautions as found in 2 Peter 1:5-10: "You must learn to know God better and discover what he wants you to do. . . . Learn to put aside your own desires so that you will become patient and godly, gladly letting God have his way with you. . . ." Baby Christians should take special care (1 Cor. 3:1-3).

Backsliding can be forgiven. God wants to forgive both sinful attitudes and ungodly practices (1 John 1:8-10).

COUNSEL

Confess your sins to God. That simply means to agree with God when he says you're wrong. Don't try to make excuses for yourself. 1 John 1:8-10 explains exactly what you must do.

Ask the Holy Spirit to take complete control, so that you can live a life which is pleasing to God (Rom. 12:1, 2; Eph. 5:18; Gal. 5:22, 23).

Determine that you're going to "grow in spiritual strength and become better acquainted with our Lord and Savior Jesus Christ" (2 Pet. 3:18).

Take the necessary steps described in 1 Corinthians 3:1-3 to keep yourself from ever backsliding again.

PRAYER

Thank God for being so patient and kind with the believer who has backslidden. Thank the Holy Spirit for faithfully convicting the believer of sin in his life. Thank the Lord Jesus Christ that his blood has now cleansed this backslider of all his sins. Pray that this believer will now begin to grow, become strong in his faith, and never backslide again.

REFERENCES

Romans 5:1, 2
Now that you are right with God you have peace with him

Romans 6:1-23
Being forgiven doesn't mean you now have a freedom to sin, but a new ability not to sin

Romans 8:1-4
Jesus has destroyed sin's control over us, so now, with the help of the Holy Spirit, we can obey God's laws

1 Corinthians 10:13
You will be tempted like anyone else, but you don't have to sin

_____

_____

_____

_____

_____

Luke 15:17, 18 (story of the prodigal son)
When he finally came to his senses, he said to himself, "At home even the hired men have food enough and to spare, and here I am, dying of hunger! I will go home to my father and say, 'Father, I have sinned against both heaven and you. . . .' "

1 John 1:8, 9
If we say that we have no sin, we are only fooling ourselves, and refusing to accept the truth. But if we confess our sins to him, he can be depended on to forgive us and to cleanse us from every wrong. . . .

Jude 24, 25
And now—all glory to him who alone is God, who saves us through Jesus Christ our Lord; yes, splendor and majesty, all power and authority are his from the beginning; his they are and his they evermore shall be. And he is able to keep you from slipping and falling away, and to bring you, sinless and perfect, into his glorious presence with mighty shouts of everlasting joy. Amen.

SCRIPTURE

Deuteronomy 11:26-28
I am giving you the choice today between God's blessing or God's curse! There will be blessing if you obey the commandments of the Lord your God which I am giving you today, and a curse if you refuse them and worship the gods of these other nations.

1 Samuel 15:22, 23
Samuel replied, "Has the Lord as much pleasure in your burnt offerings and sacrifices as in your obedience? Obedience is far better than sacrifice. He is much more interested in your listening to him than in your offering the fat of rams to him. For rebellion is as bad as the sin of witchcraft, and stubbornness is as bad as worshiping idols. And now because you have rejected the word of Jehovah, he has rejected you from being king."

Isaiah 1:19
If you will only let me help you, if you will only obey, then I will make you rich!

DESCRIPTION

Obedience is the practical acceptance of the authority and will of God, including both the inward submission and outward expression of actions, words, and thoughts of obedience to God.

BIBLICAL PERSPECTIVE

God expects obedience (Deut. 11:16-18). To choose Christ is to choose obedience (John 14:15, 16, 21). To become disobedient is to sin or rebel against God's expectations and his rights (1 Sam. 15:22, 23).

COUNSEL

To help the counselee discover areas of disobedience (either deliberate or subconscious), begin to ask questions about different areas of his life—for example, personal relationships, behavior patterns, and personal devotions.

Lead him to confess any disobedience as sin, and ask for forgiveness on the basis of Christ's atonement, claiming the promise of complete pardon. If others are involved in the disobedience, this must be addressed.

Counsel the person to plan specific actions— for example, ask forgiveness of others, make amends where needed, desire the fruit of the Spirit.

PRAYER

Pray for faithfulness to be produced in the person. Thank and praise God for revealing disobedience to us, for giving self-control to be obedient, and for giving us love for God and one another—even enemies.

REFERENCES

1 John 5:2, 3
Test of obedience and love

Colossians 3
Admonition to emulate Jesus

Psalm 51
David's example of new obedience to God

FOLLOW-UP

1. Take a piece of paper and draw a vertical line down the center.
2. To the left of the line list the areas in which you have been disobedient.
3. To the right of the line list the alternatives of obedience. Begin to act on the alternatives, forming new patterns.

John 14:15, 16, 21
If you love me, obey me; and I will ask the Father and he will give you another Comforter, and he will never leave you.

The one who obeys me is the one who loves me; and because he loves me, my Father will love him; and I will too, and I will reveal myself to him.

Luke 6:46
So why do you call me "Lord" when you won't obey me?

James 1:22
And remember, it is a message to obey, not just to listen to. So don't fool yourselves.

SCRIPTURE

Proverbs 8:12
*Wisdom and good judgment
live together, for wisdom
knows where to discover
knowledge and understand-
ing.*

James 4:6
*But he gives us more and
more strength to stand against
all such evil longings. As the
Scripture says, God gives
strength to the humble, but
sets himself against the proud
and haughty.*

Proverbs 16:5
*Pride disgusts the Lord. Take
my word for it—proud men
shall be punished.*

Proverbs 27:2
*Don't praise yourself; let
others do it!*

1 Peter 5:6
*If you will humble yourselves
under the mighty hand of
God, in his good time he will
lift you up.*

REFERENCES

Proverbs 11:2; 13:10
Pride and wisdom

1 Corinthians 1:29
No boasting before God

Philippians 2:3
Think of others as better
than yourself

Proverbs 27:2
Let others praise you

PROBLEM

The prideful person has a problem with ego—
lifting himself up at the expense of others;
lacking humility; thinking of himself above any
other (Isa. 14:13). He needs help in putting self
in proper perspective through God's eyes.

BIBLICAL PERSPECTIVE

Pride is our natural state of being, from which
issues every problem in the world. The answer
to pride is to ask for a supernatural awareness of
God and of others, which in actuality will enable
us to have genuine self-worth, as God desires us
to have (Matt. 6:33, 22:37, 39).

COUNSEL

Try to determine if the counselee is in need of
salvation in Christ. Often pride is a barrier to
true repentance.

To the counselee: In order to practice
humility, seek to mature in the fruit of the Spirit
(love, meekness). Serve others and look for
praiseworthiness in them rather than always
being critical of them. If you find yourself talking
down to others, stop and humble yourself.

PRAYER

Lead the counselee to pray for forgiveness of his
pride. Encourage him to seek Christ in prayer
and Scripture, and ask God to renew his mind in
humility and love.

FOLLOW-UP

Read daily a chapter each of Psalms and of
Proverbs.

PROBLEM

A lack of submission implies a rebellion against God and/or another person that may entail the inability to take advice or accept another person as he is (without demanding that he change his personality, habits, etc.). Lack of submission is a common problem in marriages, employer-employee relationships, and between parents and children. Christians need to face the same problems of rebellion against true submission that non-Christians do.

BIBLICAL PERSPECTIVE

The biblical injunction is to submit ourselves to God, resisting Satan, who will flee from us (James 4:7). After a person's true submission to God and his will, his other relationships can fall into proper perspectives.

COUNSEL

When the divine order of submission is followed, relationships improve and are set right; rebellion ceases and harmony follows. God's will becomes known and made sure as counsel is received from fellow Christians and one another.

As the counselee submits himself to the counselor by requesting direction and prayer (James 5:14-16), so one submits himself to God and other Christians in daily life. Encourage the counselee to search the Scriptures to memorize verses daily. This will plant God's Word in his heart so that he can become submissive. He should act on Scripture, putting it into daily practice. As prayer and praise toward God show honor and respect to him, likewise, submission to God means *to show honor and respect*. The one who *shows* honor and respect will *receive* honor and respect.

SCRIPTURE

James 4:1, 7
What is causing the quarrels and fights among you? Isn't it because there is a whole army of evil desires within you?
So give yourselves humbly to God. Resist the devil and he will flee from you.

Ephesians 5:22, 23
You wives submit to your husbands' leadership in the same way you submit to the Lord. For a husband is in charge of his wife in the same way Christ is in charge of his body the Church. (He gave his very life to take care of it and be its Savior!)

Ephesians 5:33
So again I say, a man must love his wife as a part of himself, and the wife must see to it that she deeply respects her husband—obeying, praising and honoring him.

1 Peter 3:1-4
Wives, fit in with your husbands' plans; for then if they refuse to listen when you talk to them about the Lord, they will be won by your respectful, pure behavior. Your godly lives will speak to them better than any words. Don't be concerned about the outward beauty that depends on jewelry, or beautiful clothes, or hair arrangement. Be beautiful inside, in your hearts, with the lasting charm of a gentle and quiet spirit which is so precious to God.

Ephesians 6:1-4
Children, obey your parents; this is the right thing to do because God has placed them in authority over you. Honor your father and mother. This is the first of God's Ten Commandments that ends with a promise. And this is the promise: that if you honor your father and mother, yours will be a long life, full of blessing.

And now a word to you parents. Don't keep on scolding and nagging your children, making them angry and resentful. Rather, bring them up with the loving discipline the Lord himself approves, with suggestions and godly advice.

Ephesians 6:5-9
Slaves, obey your masters; be eager to give them your very best. Serve them as you would Christ. Don't work hard only when your master is watching and then shirk when he isn't looking; work hard and with gladness all the time, as though working for Christ, doing the will of God with all your hearts. Remember, the Lord will pay you for each good thing you do, whether you are slave or free.

PRAYER

Meekness is a fruit of the Spirit that includes being submissive to God. The meek will receive the earth as an inheritance (Matt. 5:5). It is the meek to whom the earth *can* be entrusted. Pray for meekness for the counselee, as well as for goodness and kindness.

REFERENCES

James 5:14-16
Submit to prayers of others

Galatians 5:22, 23
A fruit of the Spirit is meekness

Romans 12
Especially verse 10, "take delight in honoring each other"

READING
The Calvary Road by Roy Hession
Beyond Humiliation by John G. Mantte

SEXUAL SINS

SCRIPTURE

1 Corinthians 6:9, 10
Don't you know that those doing such things have no share in the Kingdom of God? Don't fool yourselves. Those who live immoral lives, who are idol worshipers, adulterers or homosexuals—will have no share in his Kingdom. Neither will thieves or greedy people, drunkards, slanderers, or robbers.

Romans 1:21, 26, 27
Yes, they knew about him all right, but they wouldn't admit it or worship him or even thank him for all his daily care. And after awhile they began to think up silly ideas of what God was like and what he wanted them to do. The result was that their foolish minds became dark and confused.
That is why God let go of them and let them do all these evil things, so that even their women turned against God's natural plan for them and indulged in sex sin with each other. And the men, instead of having a normal sex relationship with women, burned with lust for each other, men doing shameful things with other men and, as a result, getting paid within their own souls with the penalty they so richly deserved.

PROBLEM

The sin of homosexuality involves sexual relations between two persons of the same sex, or lusting after someone of the same sex. Homosexuals are often referred to as gays (male) or lesbians (female). Homosexuality is a sin that creates tremendous emotional, physical, and social problems.

BIBLICAL PERSPECTIVE

The Word of God calls homosexuality an abomination because it is a rebellion against God's original plan of one man and one woman united together for life. Married couples are commanded to be fruitful and multiply, which is impossible for homosexual couples. Homosexuality is a serious offense which led to the death penalty for violators in the Old Testament (Lev. 18:22; 20:13).

COUNSEL

Determine whether the person is seeking salvation: show him how to become a child of God. If he is already a Christian, then the need for deliverance from sin is most urgent.

In 2 Timothy 3:3 the Bible warns us that in the last days men "will think nothing of immorality." Unless the counselee is repentant and under the conviction of the Holy Spirit, he will inevitably be angry and defensive of his life-style. Suggest to the individual that he needs to be in a position of glorifying God and that this is impossible in the midst of known sin. Encourage the counselee to forsake his past sin, seek forgiveness, and begin to move into fellowship with Christ and his church. Advise him to abstain from further association with others involved in homosexual activity. Remember that the healing of homosexuality involves dealing with the lust that creates or heightens the propensity to sin. As for homosexuals who have turned to God, Christians need to encourage them to persevere. Read 1 Thessalonians 5:14b; Galatians 6:1; 1 John 1:9.

As with other behavior, there is a pattern that leads to the homosexual act. When the pattern is known, deliberately engaging in a different pattern can lead away from the act. To recognize the pattern, start at the act and trace actions, thoughts, and routines backward to the place that marks the beginning of the pattern. An acceptable and victorious alternative can be found in acts of praise and worship.

PRAYER
In the authority of Jesus pray for the binding of lust and homosexual desire. Pray for the person to be free from sin and to find victory and newness of life in Christ through the power of the Holy Spirit.

FOLLOW-UP
The homosexual must be directed to new models through working and worshiping with heterosexual Christians who really care about him. At this point in his life he may relate only to the love of someone of the same sex and to "the act of sex." He must learn to accept working models of love without sexual connotations. Get him involved in a Christ-centered church that clearly teaches the Bible in order to learn the disciplined living required of the Christian (Rom. 6:7-23).

It is important for the person's mind to be renewed. Point to the importance of manifesting the fruit of the Spirit (Gal. 5:22, 23), saturating oneself with Scripture. We are what we think. What we think is determined by what we read, imagine, and dream. Above all, emphasize the praise principle in order to resist temptation.

1 Timothy 1:10, 11
Yes, these laws are made to identify as sinners all who are immoral and impure: homosexuals, kidnappers, liars, and all others who do things that contradict the glorious Good News of our blessed God, whose messenger I am.

Romans 6:11-14, 22
So look upon your old sin nature as dead and unresponsive to sin, and instead be alive to God, alert to him, through Jesus Christ our Lord.

Do not let sin control your puny body any longer; do not give in to its sinful desires. Do not let any part of your bodies become tools of wickedness, to be used for sinning; but give yourselves completely to God—every part of you—for you are back from death and you want to be tools in the hands of God, to be used for his good purposes. Sin need never again be your master, for now you are no longer tied to the law where sin enslaves you, but you are free under God's favor and mercy.

But now you are free from the power of sin and are slaves of God, and his benefits to you include holiness and everlasting life.

SCRIPTURE

Leviticus 18:6, 29
None of you shall marry a near relative, for I am the Lord. . . . Whoever does any of these terrible deeds shall be excommunicated from this nation.

Leviticus 20:11, 12, 14, 17
If a man sleeps with his father's wife . . . his daughter-in-law . . . with a woman and her mother . . . with his sister, the daughter of his father or of his mother, it is a shameful thing, and they shall publicly be cut off from the people of Israel. He shall bear his guilt.

Mark 6:17, 18
For Herod had sent soldiers to arrest and imprison John because he kept saying it was wrong for the king to marry Herodias, his brother Philip's wife.

1 Corinthians 5:1, 5
Everyone is talking about the terrible thing that has happened there among you, something so evil that even the heathen don't do it: you have a man in your church who is living in sin with his father's wife. . . . Cast out this man from the fellowship of the church and into Satan's hands, to punish him, in the hope that his soul will be saved when our Lord Jesus Christ returns.

PROBLEM

The sin of incest is impure sexual intercourse between close family members, whether involving two adults or an older and a younger family member. It is a crime of perverse sexual behavior. Molestation is when any older person, family member or not, sexually abuses or molests a younger, underaged person. Obvious examples would be adult-adolescent or parent-child sexual activity. The legal age of consent is normally considered in determining whether an act is one of molestation.

BIBLICAL PERSPECTIVE

Biblically, any sexual behavior outside of marriage is sinful behavior.

COUNSEL

Determine whether the counselee is the victim or the perpetrator of incest and sexual abuse.

If the counselee is the perpetrator of sexual abuse, he must repent! The pattern of his life needs to be changed by God. Counsel him to ask God to forgive him and set him free from these temptations. Direct him to a Christ-centered counselor or pastor for regular counsel. If he has not been reborn spiritually, he can be. He can have the new life God has for him (2 Cor. 5:17). The trauma of his experiences need not ruin his life from now on. Advise the counselee to "flee from temptation," and to remove himself from situations in which abuse might occur.

If the counselee is the victim of sexual abuse, he or she may feel guilty for consenting to incest or allowing the sexual abuse. Many who have been victims (willingly or not) of incest or molestation have memories that deny them the freedom to live without hate, bitterness and resentment, fear, and/or a desire for revenge. Advise the counselee that God still loves him or her, and that he wants the victim to be able to forgive. Jesus and Stephen, at the time of their deaths, were both able to forgive those who executed them. Both looked to heaven and asked God to forgive the sins of those who were guilty. If the victim is a Christian, he or she has authority and influence with God concerning remittance of sin or retention of sin (John 20:23). God will listen to the counselee's prayer. Remind him or her that Jesus came to forgive rather than to condemn (John 3:16). God will even release the victim from the pain of the memories. Encourage the victim to allow the Holy Spirit, in power and healing, to cleanse him or her and to give God's peace.

Any victim of sexual abuse needs ongoing psychological and spiritual counsel. Direct the counselee to a Christ-centered counselor and/or pastor who is firmly rooted in God's Word.

PRAYER
Encourage both the perpetrator and the victim to pray for God's forgiveness or for the ability God grants to forgive. Encourage the counselee to thank and praise God and honor him as the Problem Solver. Advise the counselee that dwelling upon the problem honors Satan and the sin. Boldly, in Jesus' name, rebuke incest as a perversion of God's intentions. Renounce the sin and the satanic influence over everyone involved.

Romans 13:14
But ask the Lord Jesus Christ to help you live as you should, and don't make plans to enjoy evil.

1 Corinthians 10:13
But remember this—the wrong desires that come into your life aren't anything new and different. Many others have faced exactly the same problems before you. And no temptation is irresistible. You can trust God to keep the temptation from becoming so strong that you can't stand up against it, for he has promised this and will do what he says. He will show you how to escape temptation's power so that you can bear up patiently against it.

REFERENCES

1 Corinthians 5:1, 6; 6:13-18; 7:2
Sexual impurity in the church

1 Thessalonians 4:3
Fornication

Proverbs 2:16-19; 6:20; 7:27; 9:13-18
Adultery

Genesis 19:1-30; Romans 1:18-32
Perversion

SCRIPTURE

Galatians 5:16-18
I advise you to obey only the Holy Spirit's instructions. He will tell you where to go and what to do, and then you won't always be doing the wrong things your evil nature wants you to. For we naturally love to do evil things that are just the opposite from the things that the Holy Spirit tells us to do; and the good things we want to do when the Spirit has his way with us are just the opposite of our natural desires. These two forces within us are constantly fighting each other to win control over us, and our wishes are never free from their pressures. When you are guided by the Holy Spirit you need no longer force yourself to obey Jewish laws.

Galatians 5:22-24
But when the Holy Spirit controls our lives he will produce this kind of fruit in us: love, joy, peace, patience, kindness, goodness, faithfulness, gentleness and self-control; and here there is no conflict with Jewish laws.

Those who belong to Christ have nailed their natural evil desires to his cross and crucified them there.

PROBLEM

Lust is desiring anything in a compelling, cunning, luring manner. Though the word is used most often for sexual desire, it encompasses all kinds of fleshly desire.

BIBLICAL PERSPECTIVE

Paul lists several works of the flesh, stating that persons who practice such works will have no part in the Kingdom of God (Gal. 5:19-21). The whole Bible witnesses to the fact that persons can, with God's help, rise above the consuming desire for such things as sex, money, possessions, and power.

COUNSEL

A person's human nature is not destroyed when the person is saved. Rather, it is atoned for and pardoned. After being born again, one can ask for temperance (that is, self-control), a fruit of the Spirit. Through the help of the Spirit, a person can gain control over lust. It must be confessed as sin and repented of in order for the counselee to be set free.

The counselee may feel that his desires are too powerful to be controlled. He needs assurance that no desire of the flesh is so powerful that God cannot subdue it. Emphasize the need to praise God and to ask for relief from unspiritual desires, believing confidently that relief will come. Emphasize also the diligent study of the Scriptures. Regular study of the Bible helps keep us mindful of God's willingness to forgive our sins and help us overcome any temptation.

PRAYER

Have the counselee pray the following: *Father, thank you for sending your Son, Jesus Christ, to help me rise above my carnal desires. Let your perfection be my perfection, and let your holiness be my holiness. I claim victory over my lust, in the name and by the power of Jesus Christ. Amen.*

REFERENCES

Galatians 5, 6
Freedom and help in Christ

1 Peter 2:11, 12
Abstaining from evil pleasures

1 Timothy 6:9, 10
Lust for money

2 Timothy 2:22, 23
Fleeing from evil thoughts

READING

Prison to Praise by Merlin Carothers
Walking and Leaping by Merlin Carothers
Answers to Praise by Merlin Carothers

Romans 6:12
Do not let sin control your puny body any longer; do not give in to its sinful desires.

1 John 2:15, 16
Stop loving this evil world and all that it offers you, for when you love these things you show that you do not really love God; for all these worldly things, these evil desires—the craze for sex, the ambition to buy everything that appeals to you, and the pride that comes from wealth and importance—these are not from God. They are from this evil world itself.

Psalm 119:11
I have thought much about your words, and stored them in my heart so that they would hold me back from sin.

SCRIPTURE

Romans 1:27, 28
And the men, instead of having a normal sex relationship with women, burned with lust for each other, men doing shameful things with other men and, as a result, getting paid within their own souls with the penalty they so richly deserved.

1 Corinthians 6:9-11
Don't you know that those doing such things have no share in the Kingdom of God? Don't fool yourselves. Those who live immoral lives, who are idol worshipers, adulterers, or homosexuals—will have no share in his Kingdom. Neither will thieves or greedy people, drunkards, slanderers, or robbers. There was a time when some of you were just like that but now your sins are washed away, and you are set apart for God, and he has accepted you because of what the Lord Jesus Christ and the Spirit of our God have done for you.

Ephesians 5:3
Let there be no sex sin, impurity or greed among you. Let no one be able to accuse you of any such things.

Hebrews 13:4
Honor your marriage and its vows, and be pure; for God will surely punish all those who are immoral or commit adultery.

PROBLEM

Immorality refers to moral behavior (not necessarily sexual) that is contrary to God's standards.

Perversion refers to misuse or abuse of sex, turning away from its proper purpose, as in, for example, homosexuality.

Adultery is sexual intercourse with a person other than one's spouse.

Fornication is sexual intercourse outside the marriage bond.

BIBLICAL PERSPECTIVE

Immorality, perversion, adultery, and fornication are works of the flesh (Gal. 5:19-21). People who engage in such practices cannot inherit the Kingdom of God. When Christians allow improper sexual drives to exist within themselves, an inner tension results. One part of the person will want to be spiritual while the other part tends toward sensuality. This results in double-mindedness (James 1:8), leading to a mind completely immersed in sin (Rom. 1:28).

COUNSEL

Disobeying God's laws will result in damage to our lives and those we involve in our sins. Contrary to what the secular culture teaches, it is impossible to involve oneself physically without also involving the spiritual nature of oneself and one's partner. Trying to deny or suppress this spiritual involvement only results in the wounding of our spirits. Thus we can be guilty of marring the spiritual core of another person. The scars resulting from this kind of involvement can be deep and long-lasting.

Overcoming temptations requires following God's plan of resisting evil. If praise is offered to

God, his peace and joy fill us, and we can be released from temptation.

Encourage the counselee to fellowship in a Christ-centered church that clearly teaches the Bible.

PRAYER

Lead the counselee to pray for forgiveness, cleansing, and strength to stand fast in God's freedom. The person may need deliverance from unclean spirits.

REFERENCES

Acts 15:20; 1 Corinthians 5:1; 6:13-18; 7:2; 1 Thessalonians 4:3
Fornication

Proverbs 2:16-19; 7:27; 9:13-18; Genesis 19:1-25; Romans 1:18-32
Perversion

FOLLOW-UP

Study the injunctions and promises from Scripture. Offer praise to God and remember that he is able to see us through temptation (1 Cor. 10:13).